Learn How To Write Books That You Will Be Proud To Sell

Thomas Kaye

ISBN 978-1-4092-3491-3
Published by Lulu
URL: http://www.ThomasKaye.com
E-mail: Thomas.k@ThomasKaye.com

To my wife, Debbie

Contents

Introduction

Writing a book is a great way to drive your businesses to a higher level. Speakers, consultants, coaches, therapists and other small business owners are learning that publishing a book is one of the most powerful marketing strategies available.

Becoming a published author could change your life often dramatically. That is because as an author, you become known as the expert in your field, whatever your field is. Clients will seek you out, ready to pay good money for your services.

There are many information products (info-products) which you can create, but a book has the greatest potential to open doors. A book can give you more recognition and professional credibility than audiotapes, CDs, videos, seminars, workshops and public speaking.

Your book can even serve as the basis for a year-long mentorship program for which individuals or groups would pay hundreds or thousands of dollars to participate.

The idea is to see your book as a business itself and as a launching pad for new business opportunities.

A published book, if done correctly, is also a great way to increase your income. You probably already know this, since you have bought this book. There are so many reasons for which you may have finally decided to write you own book, but whatever your reasons are, this book will provide all the necessary information and guidance to help you write your first book and will show you how to derive profits by selling it online.

You too, can write a book! Yes, it is easier than you might think. You don't have to come up with a great big idea. All you need for becoming a published author is your everyday life or your talents and expertise, which can form the basis of a successful book if you communicate them in a clear, compelling and organized manner.

The Internet has changed dramatically the way books are published and sold. Now, it's easier than ever to produce and sell a book without even having to leave your home or office.

While the topics covered in this book apply to paper as well as electronic books, when it comes to publishing and selling we will focus mainly on the new publishing technologies, because:

- They are new.

- They are easier.

- They are cheaper.

- They are more environment friendly.

- Everyone can use them.

A strategy that works for many is to break the whole writing and publishing process into smaller steps. This book will show you all the necessary steps you need to take for becoming a self-published author. Although many of the techniques that will be described in this book may be used by conventional authors too, the focus will be electronic publishing.

Here is what you will learn:

- How to decide what you will write about.

- How to research your subject and collect valid information.

- How to plan and organize your book.

- How to write the first draft.

- How to revise and edit the draft.

- How and where to publish your book.

- How to build a web site for your book.

- How to promote your web site AND your book.

In this book, we will focus on non-fiction writing, since non-fiction depends more on your research rather than your writing skills. Non-fiction books are also easier to sell since they are either solving a problem or provide information. In other words, almost anyone can write a non-fiction book.

When you will have completed this book, you will be able to give to your audience a book that:

- They can use and benefit from.

- Will provide real solutions to their problems.

- Presents your well documented thesis on an issue and provides another perspective for them.

Whom is this book for?

This book is intended to be used mainly by first-time authors. More experienced authors will also find it useful, since it covers many aspects of the writing, publishing and selling process.

How to read this Book

This book is not really meant to be read at once. Each chapter covers a basic step of the writing process. Therefore, taken as a systematic guide, you should move on to the next chapter only after you have finished the work described in the previous chapter.

CHAPTER 1

The E-Publishing Alternative

Introduction

How many times have you dreamed of people finding and buying your book, even before you start writing it? Probably a lot! Moreover, in how many of these times did the dream take place in a "brick-and-mortar" bookstore? Probably most of them!

Now it is the time to change that dream! Traditional publishing and traditional bookstores are exactly what the name suggests: outdated!

Do you want a chance to belong in the 70% of the authors whose books are returned by bookstores?

Do you want to wait 90 or more days before you are paid from bookstores?

If your answer to the both the above questions is "no", keep reading!

Electronic book sales have increased dramatically over the past few years because the Internet has dramatically changed the way we look for information; the way we communicate; the way we shop.

According to Forrester Research, electronic books and other information products will grow to a 10 billion dollar market over the next couple of years. This is not just a possibility. It's a reality.

What has caused this growth? How long will it last? The answer to these questions comes from the problems that electronic publishing (e-publishing) solves.

E-publishing has given two major benefits: 1) It helped to reduce the costs involved in publishing, since the author or the publisher doesn't have to print thousands copies of the book, and 2) it has helped to preserve the environment, since it makes no use of paper.

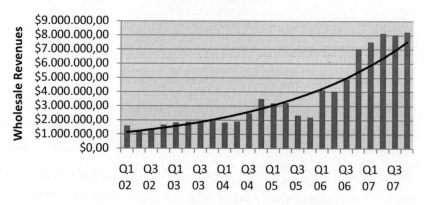

US Trade Wholesale Electronic Book Sales

Quarters 2002 through 2007

A Small History Lesson

E-publishing finds its origins back in 1971. Michael Hart was the creator of this innovation and the founder of the Project Gutenberg of Illinois University, a public library of digital books, which enjoys a collection of more than 2 thousand books, among which we find a great number of classic works.

In 1981, the first electronic book with commercial aims was launched on the market: a dictionary by Random House. However, the striking development of digital books would take place only 20 years later.

In 1998, the first Electronic-book Fair took place in Gaithersburg, Maryland in the US. At this event, the Norm Open e-book, a series of regulations to standardize the format of electronic publications, was presented. A year later the specification Open e-book Publication Structure was established, which set HTML and XML as the standard platforms for this type of books.

The electronically published books boomed when "Riding the Bullet", a Stephen King's well-known novel, was launched exclusively on the Internet in 2001. This digital work was a resounding success, with a great amount of copies sold in only 2 days at a very affordable cost-$2.50. Later, the president of Russia, Vladimir Putin, had his memories published in the same format.

From this moment on, many electronic publishers and virtual book shops with digital texts catalogues have appeared. Today, the Internet provides not only a great variety of books on sale, but also free ones, which allows great advancement of cultural dissemination. Because of the advantages that this type of publication provides, e-publishing business is expected to continue to grow in the near future.

Facts about Traditional Publishing

The following facts as they have been laid out by author Nicholas Thomas prove that e-publishing is an easier and much cheaper solution especially for first-time authors.

How are authors published? They send their manuscripts to big publishing houses for review and hope they will sign a contract to publish their book. Meanwhile, they sit around, waiting for months for the dreaded rejection notice, or even worse no notice at all. Many authors, especially first-timers are under the impression that being published by a big publisher is more prestigious. The truth is that nobody cares who publishes your book.

There is also the false impression that hiring agents to do the negotiating is an easy and sure way to be published. The truth is that you have to shop around a lot for a good agent but even then, the agent will reject well over 90% of submitted book manuscripts. On top of that, he/she will demand a healthy percentage of sales for his/her efforts. Generally, they receive a 15% commission.

Most first-time authors believe that their publisher will also promote their book. The truth is that the publisher will put up the money to manufacture the book, then his representatives will get the book into the stores and that's it. The promotion of the book is solely the author's responsibility, often at his/her own expense.

Traditional publishing takes time. It can take as long as 3 years to get a book published. Most publishers operate within an 18 month production cycle. This means that the publish date will be long after the contract has been signed.

The traditional publishing cycle has three selling seasons. This means that the book will be on the shelves for 4 months and after that, it is pulled off, so it can be replaced by other books for that season. The left over books will be sent to warehouses and they are generally sold in bulk at a fraction of the original price.

Once an author agrees to turn his/her book over to a publisher, he/she loses most or even all control of the book. Most publishing contracts, especially with new authors, give the publisher the freedom to make any changes to the book they see fit.

Many authors who don't really know all the pitfalls to being published and after many unsuccessful attempts they either give up or try to self-publish. Even though self-publishing is a good choice, there is still the necessity to gather a lot of information and approximately $13,000 to $15,000 minimum, for printing, promotion, and other expenses, of about 4000 copies of a 100 to 250 page book.

Being published can really become a daunting task and it doesn't happen overnight.

On the other hand, the electronic publishing industry is easier to join and you can do it by yourself. You don't need to be a big shot author or invest a small fortune to get started. Of course, you can't expect to make $10,000 in the first month, but the benefits of writing your own electronically published book are numerous.

Electronically published books are:

- **Easier to distribute**, compared to paper books. They don't need to be shipped in trucks and placed on shelves in bookstores. They can go straight from the writer's computer to the reader's computer. In many cases, this takes just seconds!

- **Cheaper to make**, since there are practically no costs involved for distribution, printing and binding.

- **Easier to control**, the electronic publishing revolution has truly put the author in control of his/her own product. You can submit your book to be distributed by other companies or even to be published in full. They may want to edit your content but, at the end of the day, all the decisions are yours and you have the option to distribute your book yourself.

With e-publishing, you can write just about any subject you want! Book stores will only stock certain types of books, and if your book is particularly controversial or taboo then you might not have any luck. On the Internet, however, things are different. All types of subversive materials are available and, if you so wish, you are, free to add to them.

There is no doubt that finally electronically published books will at least stand equal to print books. In addition, they have the advantage of offering numerous convenient options (like hyperlinks to web content and reference works, embedded instant shopping and ordering links, collaborative authoring, community activities, automatically or periodically updated content, multimedia capabilities, database, Favorites and History Maintenance, automatic and embedded audio conversion and translation capabilities, and more).

Benefits of Electronic Publishing for the Author

With electronic publishing you become the publisher of your own book (self-publishing) which, by definition, means that you have more control on the appearance, the marketing and promotion, the distribution and of course on the profits.

Some of the benefits of becoming an electronically published author may include:

- As the author, you receive all the profits from sales and have the potential to make a sizeable profit on each book sold.

- Electronic publishing can get your book in the market quickly especially if your book deals with a time sensitive subject.

- You can do as much or as little of the book production you want, and subcontract out the rest.

Electronic Publishing Formats

The term e-publishing is somewhat generic and may include a variety of formats. Let's look at the most important forms of electronic publishing:

Commercial E-publishing: Commercial e-publishing is very similar to commercial print publishing. Publishers decide if they will publish a book based on the quality of the book and the ability to market it. On the other hand authors do receive royalties (often as high as 40 percent), and do not have to pay anything for the production of the book. Most commercial e-publishers adapt the same process as print publishers for reviewing, editing and proofreading before publication. The books are often sold through the e-publisher's website and large online bookstores like Amazon.com and Barnes and Noble. Finally, most commercial e-publishers provide a service for obtaining ISBN numbers, copyright registration, and (sometimes) a Library of Congress listing.

Subsidy E-publishing and Print-On-Demand: Subsidy e-publishers produce and distribute books for a fee. Authors usually receive the same royalties as in commercial e-publishing (around 40 percent). Most subsidy publishers will accept any book, regardless of quality. Books are not edited or proofread and are published, "as is." Many subsidy publishers provide extra services for a fee, such as book formatting, cover design, editing and proofreading. Subsidy publishers provide no promotion. **Print-On-Demand (POD)** is another form of subsidy publishing that has become extremely popular in the last few years. In POD, the book is submitted to the publisher as an electronic file and is stored as such. When there is an order for the book, it is being sent to a commercial printer for printing and binding and then is shipped to the customer. Many POD publishers often provide an option to purchase the book as a downloadable file.

E-publishing business: How much can you expect to earn?

Creating and selling information products is a great way to earn a passive, residual income from home. It does not matter if you are a college student, a grandparent, or somewhere in between, as long as you have information in your head that people are willing to pay for. In addition to topics, you are already familiar with, it is easy to research more topics you have no prior experience with, and create information products around them.

Like in every other business your success will depend on how much effort you put in and on your product. Your success in selling your book will depend on its topic, the usefulness of its content, its price, and on how well you promote it. We will discuss all these in detail later on.

Pricing is always a difficult decision; price too high, few will buy, price to low, and you don't make much money. Most authors who are just starting generally price their products in the $20-$40 range. As their product matures and improves, higher prices can follow. An important point to remember is that selling an electronically published book requires very little overhead cost. Since there is no inventory, your only costs are related to your web site (which you may be getting free from you Internet service provider) — and any advertising costs. The rest is pure profit.

Most electronically published books contain anywhere from one hundred to five hundred pages, and sell anywhere from $10 to $100 dollars, and over, depending on the information. Let's find out in the next example how many sales you must make in order to make a profit.

Let's say that you've written a book of 5,000 to 30,000 words. It took 60 hours to write. If your rate were $60 an hour, you would make $3,600. Selling at $30 each, you'll need 120 sales to pay yourself for the time you spent writing. Almost any book you write will easily sell 120 copies. Most will sell many more.

Based on the latest researches it is safe to say that you can easily make $12,000 a year (or more) from selling your very own book. In fact, if you manage to sell just one book per day, at $34.99, you will earn $12,596 per year! By selling three self-published books per day, at $9.99 per book, you will earn $10,789 per year.

Conclusion

Electronic publishing offers possibilities for expanding access and changing learning behavior and academic research. Electronically published books would never go out of print, and new editions could be easily created and updated. Content could always be accessible, regardless of time or location of the user, and could be read on PCs or on portable book readers. An individual could carry several titles at once on a portable reader, and over the course of an academic career, build a personal library. Added functionalities include full text searching, choice of font size, and interactive functions such as mark-up, citation creation, and note taking. Print text can be integrated with multi-dimensional objects, sound, and film to create a completely new kind of monographic work.

Nick Bogaty, executive director of the International Digital Publishers Forum (IDPF, www.idpf.org) says: "I've always said that four factors need to be in place for the market to take off. You need a device that makes reading pleasurable, content at the right price, a great selection of content and books that are easy to use. We're definitely getting closer to these goals."

The Writing Process Overview

- Prewriting — Select a topic, brainstorming and planning.
- Drafting — Put your thoughts on paper, quickly.
- Revising — Examine structure and details.
- Editing — Correct spelling, grammar and style.
- Publishing — Sell your product to the world.

Prewriting

- Select a topic and **brainstorm** by jotting down all ideas on the topic as they come to mind.
- **Organize** the ideas by putting them into categories of main ideas and corresponding details.
- **Research** for information.

Drafting

- Start puting your ideas on paper as quickly as possible.
- **Don't worry about spelling and grammar.**

Revising

- Make sure you stay on topic.
- Add any supporting details.
- Delete unecessary information.
- Check the logical order of information.

Editing

- Check for spelling mistakes.
- Check for correct grammar.
- Check for correct punctuation.

Publishing

- Select Print On Demand (POD) Service.
- Make your book available at online bookstores.
- Prepare to accept payments.

CHAPTER 2

30 Idea Generation Tips

Introduction

The very first step after your decision to write a book is to find a subject to write about. So, what should you write? The easiest way to figure this out is to answer this question: **What do you love to read?** Be guided by what you love to read, not by the fact that Money Making books, cookbooks, or books on relationships are hot now. Target your books towards a very large audience. Research has shown that more than 150.000.000 people are potential online book buyers. This means that whatever the topic, you will always find people who will be interested.

1. Before you start working on your subject of choice make sure that, there is not much quality information on the Internet available free and that your target audience is willing to pay for information.

2. Don't spend all your time trying to discover a profitable niche. Pick a subject, or a topic that you like and spend this time researching on that topic. The results will be

much more rewarding.

3. The subjects of non-fiction books cover a tremendous range, and the demand for personal development and "how-to" topics has increased over the past few years. Naturally, you will be expected to have special expertise or experience in the area you want to write. This doesn't mean you have to have formal qualifications, though; relevant life experience can qualify. Most important is finding a fresh angle on the topic and performing good research.

Choosing a Subject

4. Write About What You Know: Use information or knowledge that you have already gathered (or at least partially gathered) as the basis for your book. The main issue with this approach is that it can be very hard to list all topics you already know something about. Fortunately, some innovative techniques can help you with this. You will find some in APENDIX A.

5. Do Market Research: Find topics that people are demanding information about - and supply answers. Find a "need" and solve it! Another great approach is to find first the motivating factor (see APENDIX B) which will encourage people to buy. Then work backwards, address the need and then decide on what your book will contain.

6. Do Competitive Research: Find what books people are buying right now - and enter the market yourself. It's easier this way since your competitors will already have done for you the hard work for establishing interest (educating prospects about why they should buy the products). Be a little careful though, since an already established competitor may crush you like a bug! In such

cases rather than going head-to-head against a strong competitor it may be better to find a smaller niche, and occupy it. For example if your competitor is selling a book about operating a Small Business, make yours on "Small Business Taxes", or "Small Business Marketing", or "Small Business Accounting", or any other Small Business topic on which you have sufficient expertise.

7. Generate many ideas as quickly as possible. Don't review them initially - just make a note of every single idea that you come up with. Some of the ideas will be worthless, some will be diamonds, and some will spark further ideas that might themselves be diamonds.

8. One of the best pieces of advice is to keep a pad of paper on hand at all times, even by the bed. When an idea pops into a writer's head it may not be there by the time, he sits down at the computer. Sometimes the muse strikes in the middle of the night. Eyes fly open and the brain works its magic. All writers have had that happen. Their feet hit the cold floor, hands scramble in the dark for paper and a pencil, and the idea is scrawled in the dark to be found the next morning.

Places Where Ideas Can Be Found

9. Ideas are everywhere. Good places to begin your search include bookstore shelves, conversations with family and friends, newspaper headlines, magazines, ads on television, CNN, and even junk mail. Observe people. What do they say or do? What do they eat for lunch?

10. Check the community section of the paper to find out what events are coming up. Is there a car show or art exhibition in town? Is there a city commission meeting? Attend with a note-book in hand.

11. County fairs, amusement parks and family picnics are

filled with stories. Ask people questions. Get them to tell stories from their own lives.

12. Watch the Discovery or History Channel.

13. Read the Yellow Pages of the phone book.

14. Look through old journals or diaries.

15. Movies can generate an interest in a particular subject that could grow into book ideas.

16. Ideas can also come from children's books. Look through them. Choose one line from each one and write a story based on that line.

17. Join discussion groups or question and answer groups, like Yahoo! Answers, and you will find that many people are discussing and/or asking the same questions. If people are asking about it, it likely means there is a need for more information on that topic! Here are a few things you should look for:

    • Repeat problems – Go through boards and count the number of times a question is asked. Keep tally on a piece of paper. This will come in helpful when you review your notes.

    • Questions and answers related to new products, strategies, or other innovations in your field – These are valuable because they have not been written about or explored.

18. Some great websites out there provide useful information about what is currently considered a hot topic. You can write a book on one of these topics that are highly searched for, providing some type of a unique angle and you can be sure you will find reader interest. If people need that information, they may well be almost ready to buy an Information Product on that exact topic.

- Yahoo! Buzz, (http://buzz.yahoo.com/)

- Google Zeitgeist, (http://www.google.com/press/zeitgeist.html) or Google HotTrends, (http://www.google.com/trends/hottrends)

- DogPile SearchSpy, (http://www.dogpile.com/info.dogpl/searchspy/)

- MSN A-List, (http://a-list.msn.com/)

- Zeitgeist on 43 Things, (http://www.43things.com/zeitgeist) this is indeed a great website. People are actually saying what they want to do!

- Dummies.com, (http://www.dummies.com), they are the publishers of the famous book series "for dummies". All of their topics are generated after great research and they are almost guaranteed to be in demand.

19. Find out what sells the most at online bookstores. Take one of the best selling topics, narrow it down or provide a different angle.

   - Amazon Bestsellers, (http://www.amazon.com/gp/bestsellers/books/)

   - EBay Pulse, (http://pulse.ebay.com), Category Books

Generating Topic Ideas

20. Don't get bogged down looking at the blank screen, take a walk, go to a coffee shop, or relax in the back yard. The possibilities are endless.

21. Brainstorm ideas. Turn one idea into many by writing down a topic, such as "Pets." Then, write down twenty

titles that could be written about pets. Keep adding to
the list until there are twenty prospective titles. If the list
is only four or five ideas, go to coffee with friends and get
their ideas. Make a list of interests and hobbies. What issues are most exciting? For example,

- What dog makes the best pet for children?

- What kind of fish live the longest in a tank?

- How do you train an older dog?

22. Often ideas can be generated from answering "what if"
questions.

- What if the South had won the Civil War? What
could have happened?

- What if Lincoln had lived?

- What if Columbus had perished before returning
to Spain?

- What if the US had not won the Revolutionary
War?

23. If you can't come up with any ideas write down all the
thoughts that are interfering with your thoughts about
what to write.

24. Combine search terms with each of the following to generate possible titles:

- How To _____

- Learn How To _____

- A Beginner's Guide To _____

- An Expert's Guide To _____

- Teach Yourself To _____

- It's Easy To _____

- Step-by-Step Guide To _____
- 99 (or any other number) Tips About _____
- Making (Extra) Money
- Saving Money
- Saving Time
- A Complete Guide To _____
- Little Known (Secrets) Facts About _____

25. Ask family and friends what things they would like to read about, then do a bit of research and write about it. Be sure to send that person a copy of your book once it is published.

26. Refresh or expand an existing or old subject/topic that needs fresh and updated information. Sometimes information changes, and when that happens, a follow up that talks about these changes can renew people's interest to the subject, brand the writer as an expert who keeps up to date on his topics, and bring new readers to the older content again too. If the information hasn't changed, consider writing a new book that expands or adds to the existing book(s), providing additional information on the same subject.

27. If at some point, you (the writer) had to search for information for yourself, chances are that someone else would be searching for it too. You can write a book on that subject. People use the internet to look for information on just about everything these days. Whether it's information about a new drug, how to do something, where to buy something…

28. Read! When stuck and unsure of what to write about, simple start by finding a favorite content site and start reading. It won't take long before an article or someone

else's opinion sparks that creative urge to respond, either agreeing or disagreeing, and instead of responding, write a book about it.

Evaluating Topic Ideas – Choosing a Winner!

29. Narrow down your idea list by applying filters to them.

- First Idea Filter – Go through your list of ideas and strike the ones that with the more "No" answers to the filter questions:

   o Are you interested in this topic? If you're not sufficiently interested, you may get bored soon, and have trouble finishing your book. Even if you can force yourself to finish a book about a "boring" topic, your lack of enthusiasm will show both in the content, and your sales pitch.

   o Do you know enough about this topic? If not, are you willing to learn more (research) the topic? If you have already gathered information on the topic (if the topic is a subject that really excites you) then you may have tons of material or at least Internet Bookmarks) so you don't have to spend much time on research.

   o Can you find motivating factors that will motivate people to buy? People will buy products that deliver the solutions they want or need. Look at APENDIX B, for a list of factors that motivate people to buy.

   o Can you reach people who are interested in this topic? If you know how to reach prospective customers already, this is a huge advantage. Perhaps you already know an Ezine or Web Site about the topic, so you already have a list of prospects! On the other hand if you don't know how to reach prospects, your task is not necessarily impossible, but you will need to spend more time, effort, and possibly some money on marketing.

- Second Idea Filter – Narrow down your list further by striking the remaining ideas by applying this second Idea Filter.

  o Don't pick something big and obvious. The first book that deals with any important topic—the last war, the current big business success, the next medical breakthrough—has a better chance to be successful even to the point of becoming a bestseller. If you decide to deal with the same topic, you should be aware that the problem with big, well-known topics is fact that they are well-known. It's better to leave the big topics to the big writers.

  o Find your own space. Staying away from the big topics means that you need to find your own space. If you write about things that have already been written there is a chance that people will easily respond to your book with the feeling, "Well, yes, but hasn't [insert name of well-known, bestselling writer here] already done that?" By innovating, however, you will find your own empty space—a niche that isn't already occupied by some successful author. Fortunately, you often don't need to be wildly innovative to create the illusion of existing in a new space. Incremental innovation usually works well.

Your innovation though, can't be to "write a better book." Moreover, it's not that writing a better book isn't a good idea. It's just that "writing a better book" isn't innovative. Too many writers have already thought of that idea.

o Test the market appeal of your idea. This is a quick and dirty trick to help you filter your ideas: Write a press release for your idea to verify that the book will sell well as a concept. A press release is a one-page news story that announces your book and proves to people that it's special and unique and worth looking at. Your press release gives your book a chance to break out from the pack of other books and get noticed. You can see what book press releases look like by visiting publisher web sites. While you're doing this, look at any magazines that review books: Publishers Weekly, Library Journal, Booklist, and so on. Get ideas about the sorts of books get people talking.

o Build a list of periodicals that will blurb your book. You ought to be able to come up with a list of special interest periodicals (magazines, newsletters, newspapers, and so forth) which prove that people are interested in the topic of your book. If you want to write a book about raising Guinea pigs, conspiracy theories concerning the last president, or monetary policy in emerging economies, for example, one of the best ways you can confidently predict people will buy and read your book is to verify that people are already buying and reading periodicals about the topic.

o Focus on a smaller niche. For example, instead of writing a book about "vacation tips" focus your attention on a much more targeted audience such as "vacation tips for travelers to Greek islands and beaches" or something along those lines. "Vacation tips" and information on any other broad topic, can be found free on a countless number of websites, while the topic of "vacation tips for travelers to Greek islands and beaches" is much more specific and will attract that specific demographic. When it comes to general information, people can surf the net and find all the fluff and filler they could ever handle, but when they are looking for very specific information, they will be willing to pay a premium for the information in your book instead of piecing it together from many different sources. This holds true with virtually any topic you chose. Don't worry about slicing the market too small. Focus on an audience of around 200,000 to 700,000.

o Verify your idea is big enough for a book. This is very important! You need to make sure that your idea is big enough for a book—the content you'll create should be able to fill at least 120 - 150 pages. Experienced authors can do this intuitively. However, new writers often can't gauge this very well. Especially for nonfiction books, you ought to try writing a couple of example chapters—maybe chapters 1 and 4—to make sure you have a big topic. Your chapters don't need to be perfect at this point. You just want to make sure that you can write a couple of good, rich chapters that aren't redundant. When you finish those chapters, look at rest of the research material that you have collected along with other topics that you want to cover in your book and make sure that you have enough for at least two or three more chapters that are interesting.

Conclusion

30. Keep an Idea Book. Follow the example of many professional writers who keep an "idea book" as a place to store their ideas and let them incubate. Think of this as a scrapbook rather than as a diary or journal. In your Idea Book, you can store newspaper clippings, magazine articles, personal letters, snapshots, postcards and other items that can serve as the seeds for a future title.

124 Hot Topics

This is a list of 124 Hot Topics for "How to" books, courses and information products based on highly searched key words on the internet. However, you should not use them as they are. They are intended to provide ideas for further research, using the methods already described.

1.	Advertising	43.	Home Finances	85.	Relationships
2.	Alcoholism	44.	Home Maintenance	86.	Retirement
3.	Arts and Crafts	45.	Home Remodeling	87.	Romance
4.	Auto Mechanics	46.	Home Schooling	88.	Rose Garden
5.	Auto Restoration	47.	How to Choose a College	89.	Sales/Sales Training
6.	Baby Showers	48.	How to Find a Job	90.	Scripting
7.	Baby's First Year	49.	How to Get Out of Dept	91.	Self Defense
8.	Become a Chef	50.	How to Give a Massage	92.	Self Improvement
9.	Blogging	51.	How to Pick-Up Women	93.	Selling on EBay
10.	Body Building	52.	How to Speak in Public	94.	Sewing Tips
11.	Buying Classic Cars	53.	How to Write a Resume	95.	Sex – Sexual Health
12.	Canning	54.	Income Opportunities	96.	Sign Language
13.	Caring for the Elderly	55.	Interior Design	97.	Single Fathers
14.	Carpentry	56.	Internet	98.	Single Mothers
15.	Catering	57.	Internet Auctions	99.	Skin Care
16.	Child Development	58.	Internet Business	100.	Sleep Remedies
17.	Coaching	59.	Internet Marketing	101.	Small Appliance Repair
18.	Computer Maintenance	60.	Investments	102.	Social Networks
19.	Computer Programming	61.	Learn Martial Arts	103.	Software
20.	Computer Repair	62.	Low Carb Recipes	104.	Speed Reading
21.	Computer Software	63.	Make More Money	105.	Stocks
22.	Cooking	64.	Makeup	106.	Stop Smoking
23.	Copywriting	65.	Marketing	107.	Success
24.	Dating	66.	Menopause	108.	Suicide
25.	Divorce	67.	Natural Remedies	109.	Tantric Sex
26.	Dog Training	68.	Obesity	110.	Tattoos
27.	Dream Interpretation	69.	Online Dating	111.	Teenage Fathers
28.	Drug Addiction	70.	Parenting	112.	Teenage Mothers
29.	E-books	71.	Party Games for Kids	113.	Teenagers
30.	Exercise	72.	Pet Care	114.	Terrorism
31.	Flowers	73.	Pet Grooming	115.	Throwing a Party
32.	Foreign Languages	74.	Pet Shows	116.	Time Management
33.	Gardening	75.	Photography	117.	Traveling
34.	Goal Setting	76.	Pilates	118.	Web Design
35.	Graphic Design	77.	Planning a Conference	119.	Wedding Planning
36.	Headaches	78.	Planning a Seminar	120.	Weight Loss
37.	Health and Fitness	79.	Plastic Surgery	121.	Weight Training
38.	Healthy Eating	80.	Plumbing	122.	Wine Testing
39.	Herbs	81.	Rape Prevention	123.	Women's Fitness
40.	Home Business	82.	Real Estate	124.	Work at Home
41.	Home Buying	83.	Recipes		
42.	Home Decoration	84.	Reflexology		

CHAPTER 3

22 Research Tips

Introduction

Research is the MOST important part of the writing process. Proper research will help you provide accurate and up-to-date information, which will be useful to your readers and increase your credibility!

1. Research must be done before you start writing!

2. Your research should aim to:

    - Collect the basic information that will go into your book.

    - Check the information that will go into your book is factually correct.

    - Check the information that will go into your book is up to date.

3. When collecting the research material, you should:

    - Keep all electronic files that you collect for each

book, in separate folders.

- Bookmark any useful web sites and organize your bookmarks logically.

- Not forget to use offline resources - like books and libraries!

- Keep a file of any photocopies, newspapers cuttings, etc., that form part of your research efforts.

4. Organize the collected material according to your book outline. You may also find that some the collected material will not be immediately usable. Make an effort not to delete anything at this point, since you don't know if it will be useful later on.

5. Research material is meant as an aid for your own writing. Do not copy or plagiarize other people's work. The only case where it's okay to use somebody else's work - is when you have permission from the copyright holder (usually the author).

Common Mistakes Made During Research

6. Avoid making the following mistakes during your research:

- Rely only on Internet searches for your research and ignore other key sources.

- Do not critically evaluate the quality of the information you find.

- Copy information from the Internet and don't acknowledge their sources.

Where to Find Information

7. **Interviews** - The first rule of interviewing would be to find an expert. The second rule is to develop your listen-

Types of Sources:

Primary Sources

▶ Original documents with no interpretation, evaluation, or analysis

▶ Original documents created contemporaneously with the event under discussion

▶ Reflects the individual viewpoint of a participant or observer.

▶ Usually found in library or manuscript collections. Many have also been copied onto microfilm, published, reissued, translated, or, in some instances, published digitally on the web.

▶ The research librarians can assist you in locating primary sources.

Examples of primary sources:

▶ Books, magazines and newspaper articles published at the time

▶ Speeches, interviews, letters, memoirs, autobiographies

▶ Public opinion polls

▶ Artifacts of all kinds: physical objects, furniture, tools, clothing, etc.

▶ Photographs, audio recordings, movies and videos

Secondary Sources

▶ Sources that interpret, evaluate, or analyze a primary source

▶ At least one step removed from the event.

Examples of secondary sources:

▶ Articles in scholarly journals that interpret literary or art works, historical events or persons.

▶ Commentaries and annotations accompanying the primary sources in the same volume. These are often referred to as critical editions.

▶ Books summarizing, synthesizing, or retelling historical events

▶ Biographies, critical works, commentaries

Tertiary Sources

▶ Sources that compile, summarize, digest, or index secondary sources

Examples of tertiary sources:

▶ Print or online indexing and abstracting resources, such as: Sociological Abstracts, MLA Bibliography, PsychInfo, Expanded Academic Index

▶ Reference works, such as encyclopedias, dictionaries, atlases, handbooks, chronologies

▶ Book-length bibliographies

ing skills. If you don't understand what you're hearing, ask for clarifications. Summarize, in your own words, what you understood.

8. **Public, University and Specialized Library** - Your best

friend should be the research librarian at your local library. Before everything was computerized, librarians acted as walking databases. No matter what you asked them, they could point you to the area of the room, the shelf, and the precise reference book you needed. Ninety percent of research is done through libraries' full-text databases. Most universities have a large, central library and several special-collection libraries. These often include art and architecture, business, all branches of science, law, medicine, music, and special collections; but many large universities have even more.

9. **Other Books on your subject** – There is no such thing as a new idea. Chances are that if you have thought of it, someone else has, too; and that person has probably written a book about it. That doesn't mean you should abandon your idea; it simply means you must tackle it in a different way.

10. **Corporations** – One of the best ways to learn about a specific industry or publicly held company within that industry is to start collecting annual reports from a stockbroker or directly from the company. Then look up relevant magazine and newspaper articles. You may also check out business publications, such as The Wall Street Journal, Business Week, Forbes, Fortune, and Barron's, and business-related TV channels.

11. **Government agencies** - There is so much literature put out by government agencies. It is there for the asking, and most of it is free of charge. Besides departments and major agencies, there are boards, commissions, committees, offices, and services, as well as judicial, legislative, and administrative sources.

12. **The Internet** - In today's world, the World Wide Web is an unlimited source of informational material. The secret

of researching on the Web is to know how to use search engines. We would look into that further on.

13. Most of the times, it will be impossible to use all the above sources. Try to use as many sources as possible and never settle for just one or two sources.

How to Evaluate Sources

14. If you intend to rely on a book, article, pamphlet, web site, or any other source for your research you need to make sure it fits your needs, contains updated and valid information.

15. When evaluating print sources check the following:

   - Who is the author?
   - Are the author's credentials (education or experience) related to the subject?
   - Does the information seem current? What is the copyright date?
   - Are statements or ideas supported by references, notes or citations (look at bibliographies) that can be checked?
   - Does the material seem to be targeting a specific audience (students, academics, business persons, public)?
   - Can you determine if the material is scholarly or popular?
   - Can you detect bias in the information provided?

16. When evaluating web sources check the following (The following points are a general approach to evaluating web resources. For a more detailed approach, please check APPENDIX C – Evaluating Web Resources).

- What is the URL type? (.com/.edu/.org/.gov/ .mil/.us/~, etc.)? Keep in mind if the site is a ".com" the creator(s) of the web site are probably trying to sell you something.

- Who is the author? Is an e-mail address or contact information provided? Are there any other clues to the author's qualifications such as a biography or hyperlink? Is there an "about us" feature?

- Are the author's credentials (education or experience) related to the subject?

- Does the information seem current? Is there a date given when the page was created? Is there a "last updated" entry?

- Are statements or ideas supported by references, notes or citations that can be checked? (Look for a bibliography or a list of resources used).

- Does the material seem to be targeting a specific audience (students, academics, business persons, public)?

- What is the purpose of the web site? Is it to inform, persuade, sell, share, or explain?

- Are there links to other web sites with other opinions? Are the links evaluated or annotated in any way?

- Can the information be validated by another credible source? Which one?

- Can you detect bias in the information given?

Research Plan

17. Before you begin your research, it is important to have a

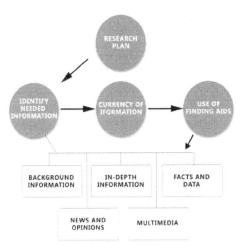

plan. The minimum required steps to building a successful research plan is to: 1) Decide on what type of information you may need, 2) Consider how current the information should be and 3) The use of finding aids to help locate information sources.

18. Divide your research in to major topics, which could possibly be the chapters' titles and sub-topics, which would serve as the chapters' key points. For every major topic or sub-topic try to find answers to all or most of the "Journalist's Questions" – Who, What, When, Where, Why and How. This way you will approach the subject from different angles that will eventually lead to well written book.

How to Keep Things Organized

19. It is very important to have a system that helps you take notes and keep track of all your collected information.

20. Create a folder on your computer with the title of your book. Inside that folder, create folders for each chapter.

Label them with the chapters' titles or, for simplicity's sake, Chapter 1, 2, 3, etc. Then, label a set of cardboard folders exactly the same way. Keep the headings simple so you can easily remember them. Everything that goes in your electronic files should have a duplicate in your paper files and vice-versa.

21. Every time you make a note, be sure to write down all bibliographic information to include author, book title, article title, page numbers, volume number, publisher name, web site information and dates. Write this information on every file and/or photocopy. This is critical!

22. Save your work often, and ALWAYS back up all your files.

CHAPTER 4

56 Writing Tips

Introduction

The first thing you must understand is that the act of writing is personal and is not something that could be taught. The guidelines that will be described in this chapter will help you produce something that people will actually read.

How to Pick a Title

1. The title of your book should accomplish two things:

    - Give to the reader a basic description of what the book is about.

    - Capture the reader's attention.

2. **Rule #1**: If your potential buyer has to ask the question "What is this book about?" after reading the title then you have the wrong title. If your potential buyer thinks, "I want to read this book", then you are on the right track.

3. You have probably heard the expression "You will never have a second chance to make a good first impression".

The same expression applies to book titles. Imagine your book in a bookshelf or in an electronic bookstore among tens or hundreds other titles on the same subject. If the title doesn't get the reader's attention immediately, you will lose the sale.

4. A great example on how the title affects book sales is Dale Carnegie's textbook "How to Win Friends and Influence People." Dale Carnegie wrote this book in 1937. It outsold every book ever written, except the Bible. The book's title, in addition to perfect timing (right after the Depression), has **TWO BENEFITS**: Winning friends— **and** influencing people. Carnegie followed with another book: "How to Stop Worrying and Start Living," another best seller, also with two benefits in the title. Who in this life does not want to stop worrying or start living?

5. **Rule #2**: Offer specific benefits that will appeal to your audience. The challenge is to meet or beat the perceived needs or wants of the audience. The title must satisfy a want, meet a need, answer a question or fulfill a curiosity. What benefit does your book offer your audience? Will it help them grow hair, lose weight, improve their love life, get more freedom, make a difference or make more money?

6. Here's some easy homework: Buy a copy of the National Enquirer and Reader's Digest. These two publications are outstanding examples, each with dozens of titles that sell. Study the titles and the content, then the titles once again. Analyze what makes them work.

7. **Rule #3**: If you do a search in your local library, you will find thousands of books whose titles begin with "How to." Consider making your book's title catchier by starting it with "How to ..."

8. **Rule #4**: Use numbers. Anyone who has worked on a

women's magazine knows that numbers work well in cover lines - **50 new ways with hair** or **346 new looks for summer.** Numbers do seem to work well in book titles also - at least they have for author Elliot Perlman. His first novel was called *Three Dollars*, and his second was called *Seven Types of Ambiguity.* However, the origins of both titles are based, in the first case, on the author's personal experience of having just that amount of money left in his own account on the day he started writing the book. In the second case, he makes a direct reference and homage to an influential work of criticism by William Empson.

9. **Rule #5**: Get your friends or family involved. Ask them to rate your potential book titles and tell you why they rated the way they did. You could also ask them to tell you their ideas on how to make your title more attractive.

10. **Rule #6**: Benefits! They are the key to a great book title. Offer your audience lots of benefits.

How to Create the Outline

The outline is a concise overview of the whole book. Consider it as the working plan for your book. During this stage, keep working with your research notes until that overview is achieved.

11. Taking the time to write a book outline can mean the difference between writing a high quality book and writing a book that winds up in the bargain bin.

12. Writing a book outline will keep your writing process focused and organized.

13. Before you start working on the outline, determine your book's thesis as well as its audience and purpose. In a nonfiction book, all parts of the outline should be con-

structed and organized to support your thesis or central point. Therefore, you have to have a sense of what you will argue in the book.

14. Decide on your main categories. The main categories are the key points of your thesis or statement, which indicate the main chapters of your book.

15. Put your main categories in a logical order. This will be the order that they will appear in your book. You may use chronological or thematical order, but whatever you choose make sure it makes sense.

16. Label each main category with a Roman numeral (i.e. "I.", "II.", "III.", etc.) or a number (i.e. "1.0", "2.0", "3.0," etc.).

17. Fill in the subcategories for each main category. These will be the sub-topics of your chapters or their main headings.

18. Label each subcategory with a letter ("A." "B.", "C.", etc.) or with a decimal. (i.e. for main category "1." the first subcategory would be "1.1", and the next would be "1.2". The first subcategory under main category 2 would be "2.1" and so on).

19. Fill in the tertiary categories. Within each subcategory, list and arrange your specific notes to support or expand the argument or point made on that subcategory.

20. If you are using Roman numeral outlines, label each tertiary category as a number. Therefore, you would have "1.", "2.", "3.", etc. If you are using the decimal outline, label each tertiary category as a decimal with two decimal points. (i.e. "1.1.1", "1.1.2", "1.2.1" and so on).

21. Continue by adding smaller divisions as needed. While tertiary categories are often sufficient, many outlines may

require smaller divisions.

10 Qualities
of a Good Non-Fiction Book

1. The book makes clear statements.

2. The writer shows a strong understanding of the topic and source material used.

3. There is evidence that the writer has read widely on the topic, including the recognized authorities in the field.

4. The book acknowledges the opposition but shows why the point being argued is more valid.

5. The points are organized in a clear and logical way.

6. Each point is supported by solid, persuasive facts and examples.

7. Every outside source is carefully documented.

8. All supporting material can be verified.

9. The book follows the standard conventions of the genre, including the use of correct documentation and a Works Cited page.

10. The book uses standard written English (or any other language that you may want to use, depending on your target audience).

22. In most cases, the major topics from your index cards will form the titles of your book's chapters and the sub-topics the major headings inside the chapters.

23. The outline does not need to be firm and it is better to be left flexible. In this initial stage of organization, the goal is simply to move from loosely ordered notes to something linear, thematic and direct. Something that makes it easier to see which thoughts and ideas are no longer appropriate and should be cut, which parts of the book are well thought through or thinly developed, and what other possibilities there may be for the book's overall structure.

24. The easiest way to outline your book is to use index cards. Go through all your notes and research material and write on the index cards a small summary (one or two sentences) for each one of your notes. Next, arrange the index cards in a logical sequence. Once you are happy with the result, write the sentences on a piece of paper as they appear on your layout. This is your book outline.

25. Save any unused material, somewhere in case you want to go back to it later for inspiration or to confirm that there is nothing usable.

26. If you can't figure out what level (i.e. main, subcategory, or tertiary) a given point should be, ask yourself whether that point adds something completely new or different to the book or whether it simply supports or explains a point or argument that is already there. If it supports or explains an existing category, it should be listed as a smaller division of that category.

27. Once you have finished the outline you may begin writing your book.

The Draft

28. Begin your writing by drafting your book. The draft, is your initial attempt to organize your thoughts in prose writing, is more complete than an outline and elaborates

your ideas in complete sentences and paragraphs.

29. Focus on getting your ideas down in a way that reflects your outline.

30. Focus on the content. As you write, you will discover ways to improve your content and even your outline. You may decide to move, delete, or add sections. In other words, you will find that your draft is another stage of thinking in writing. As you refine your ideas about your book, keep in mind that too many changes will impede your progress; if the change seems worthwhile, however, don't hesitate to change direction.

31. When you write the first draft of your book:

   - Write as much as you can as quickly as you can.

   - Don't worry about grammar, phrasing, repetition, etc.

   - Don't worry at all about layout or getting stuff into the right program - just write in your word processor or whichever program you can use most easily.

Sentences

32. Sentences should not be more than about three or four clauses long.

33. The longer a sentence becomes, the more difficult it is to keep it in your head all at once, and it will be hard for your reader to understand you.

Paragraphs

34. Open any book or newspaper, and you'll see right away that the text is divided into paragraphs. Essentially, your job in the drafting process is to translate your outline—along with other good ideas, you have along the way—

into paragraphs.

35. Begin your paragraphs with a topic sentence. The topic sentence tells the reader the main idea of the paragraph.

36. All the sentences in the paragraph should relate to one main idea. Do your reader a favor and make it clear what your main idea is—this will avoid misunderstandings.

37. Coherent paragraphs flow from sentence to sentence. This means that the sentences are linked to each other logically. You might organize the sentences in a paragraph according to chronological or sequential order, by cause and effect, by comparison and contrast, in order of degree, or in spatial order.

38. Good paragraphs include details that support the main idea. Supporting details include anecdotes, examples, facts, opinions, quotations, and/or statistics that back up the paragraph's main idea.

About Style

39. Style refers to how something is written. Choosing the best style for your book is like deciding what to wear. You wouldn't use the same language for every situation. It all depends on what the book is about and who is your book's intended audience.

40. No one - not even this book - can tell you what your writing style is or what it should be. As you become a better writer, you will develop your own style that feels comfortable and comes to you naturally. Only you can find your own style and this will take time and practice.

41. Writing is all about making choices. Style boils down to three factors: word choice, voice and sentence structure. However, how do you know what style is right for a particular book? The answer is to go back and look again, at

what your book is trying to accomplish. If your book is mainly set out to **entertain**, you need to ask what style will be the most entertaining. If your book is set out to **persuade**, you need to ask what style will be most persuasive. If you're set out to **inform**, you need to ask what style will be best to convey information.

42. When you are trying to **entertain** your reader you can write in whatever style you want, from super-formal to very slangy—whatever you think will be most "entertaining". An informal style, with casual, everyday words written in a first person voice, usually will do the trick. In addition, you want to keep the sentences simple, but not childish.

STYLE EXAMPLES

JARGON, VERY FORMAL.
Consequent to the appreciation in the exchange value of Sterling against other currencies, necessary fiscal measures were introduced by the government in order to reduce the likelihood of an import-led consumer spending surge.

This is the style of language used in official reports, technical studies, etc. It is exclusively a style of written English, full of verbal nouns, technical words and passives.

WRITTEN, FORMAL, CLEAR.
After the international value of Sterling rose, the government was obliged to take fiscal measures to reduce the likelihood of a surge in consumer spending led by cheaper imports.

This is clear, written English, as found in the press or in documents aimed at ordinary educated readers.

WRITTEN STYLE FOR THE GENERAL PUBLIC, DISCOURSE, SCRIPTED RADIO OR TV NEWS STYLE.
As the value of Sterling increased compared to other currencies, the government was forced to take tax measures to head off a rapid increase in consumer spending spurred on by cheaper imports.

FORMAL SPOKEN STYLE – RADIO, SEMINAR, TALK.
As Sterling's international value went up, the government had to take tax measures to head off a consumer spending boom spurred on by cheaper imports.

RELAXED, INFORMAL SPOKEN STYLE: DISCUSSION.
As Sterling went up in value, the government had to put up taxes to stop consumers splashing out on too many cheap imports.

There is plenty of use of prepositional verbs. All actions are now expressed through verbs, not verbal nouns.

43. When you are trying to **persuade** or **inform** your reader, you want to choose a style that makes your writing as persuasive or informative as possible. You want to sound as if you know what you are talking about, and that you

have a considered, logical view rather than an emotional response. Even when you are taking sides and putting forward an argument, you will be basing it on logic, not emotion.

44. A sense of authority is best achieved by a fairly formal and impersonal style. You would probably choose:

- reasonably formal words (not pompous ones, though);
- no slang or colloquial words;
- no highly emotional or prejudiced language;
- third-person or passive voice (no 'I');
- grammatically correct sentences, not too simple (but not too tangled, either).

How to Convince Your Readers

45. In order to convince your readers and build your reader's confidence in the ideas that you express, you must establish your credibility, make a good argument and explain your reasoning.

46. To establish your credibility you must put yourself in your readers' shoes. Think about the background, assumptions, and point of view of your reader.

- Try to anticipate objections and questions that will pop into your reader's mind as he or she reads your book.
- Be honest. Don't put forth claims you can't back up. Don't make up stuff that's not true.
- Don't exaggerate.
- Use other experts' opinions to support your ideas. Experience and prestigious reputations usually

mean greater credibility. Make sure your sources are credible. Not all expert opinions are equally credible.

- Try to avoid bias.

- Do not offend your audience. Be sensitive in your choice of words and in the ways you characterize others. Show respect for other cultures and opinions even if you do not agree with them.

- Try to avoid making absolute statements. Absolute statements include the words all, always, never, none, and so on. Use these words very carefully.

47. How to make a convincing argument to persuade your readers:

- Introduce and explain the issue. Your reader may or may not be familiar with the issue. If they are not, you need to provide a balanced overview of it. Even if they are familiar with the issue, they will judge your credibility by how you define the issue.

- Take a stand. Tell your reader where you stand on the issue. Usually this is done in your thesis statement.

- Tell your reader why they should agree with you or why they should support your cause. Use specific evidence: facts, quotations, statistics, and so on.

- Refute opposing arguments. Tell your reader why the other side is misguided, or why your position makes more sense.

- Concede the valid points of other positions. Don't try to ignore or hide the facts when they aren't on your side.

- Conclude logically. Show how your conclusion

stems logically from your position and the evidence you've provided.

48. To strengthen your writing you need to explain and support the reasons you give for your position. This is how:

- Show the progression of your argument as you write.

- Give strong examples and details that support your position.

- Explain how your examples and supporting details relate to your argument.

Beginning and Ending Your Book

49. The introduction and conclusion are perhaps the most important parts of your book. You want to make a good first impression in the introduction. Remember you only have about four to five pages before your reader decides to keep reading or not. On the other hand, the purpose of the conclusion is to leave your reader with a favorable impression and your message.

50. In the introduction to your book, you clearly tell your reader what your book is about.

51. The two main goals of the introduction are:

- Get your reader's attention.

- Present and explain your main argument.

52. To get your reader's attention, consider beginning your introduction with one of the following:

- Interesting or surprising facts

- A vivid description

- A question

- An anecdote

- A quotation

- A stance on an issue

53. On the other hand, your conclusion is your last opportunity to tell your reader your message. It's usually the last thing he or she will read. Your conclusion should accomplish these goals:

   - Remind your reader of your thesis statement.

   - Summarize the main ideas of your book.

   - Give your reader a take-home message. A take-home message is the most important message you would like your readers to keep. One way to come up with your take-home message is to ask yourself this question: "If I could choose only one thing for my reader to remember, take home, and share with others, what would it be?" This is the message you want to include in your conclusion.

54. Here are some ways to conclude your book:

   - Spur the reader to action

   - Suggest a course of action

   - Generalize to a broader situation

   - Make a prediction about the future

   - Ask your reader a question

   - Use a thoughtful quotation or anecdote

Formatting the Chapters

55. In order to keep your readers reading and not get tired because they feel lost, you need to have a consistent format of your book's chapters. This format will also pro-

vide the framework for each chapter.

56. A general structure of the book's chapters should consist of the following elements:

- **Chapter Title and Subtitle:** Each chapter title should be concise and informative. Chapter titles are often used to market the book, and many prospective readers skim these titles to determine if a book is worth reading.

- **Abstract**: The abstract of 100-150 words should clearly summarize the objectives and content of the chapter. As an alternative, you may write a quote from someone famous or an expert in the field.

- **Introduction**: Describe the general perspective of this chapter.

- **Background**: Provide broad definitions and discussions of the topic and incorporate views of others (literature review) into the discussion to support, refute or demonstrate your position on the topic.

- **Main Text of the Chapter**:

  o Issues, Controversies, Problems - Present your perspective on the issues, controversies, problems, etc., as they relate to the theme and arguments supporting your position. Compare and contrast with what has been, or is currently being done as it relates to your specific topic and the main theme of the book.

  o Solutions and Recommendations - Discuss solutions and recommendations in dealing with the issues, controversies, or problems presented in the preceding section.

- o Future Trends - Discuss future and emerging trends. Provide insight about the future of the book's theme from the perspective of your topic. Viability of a paradigm, model, implementation issues of proposed programs, etc. may be included in this section. If appropriate, suggest future research opportunities within the domain of the topic.

- **Conclusion**: Provide a discussion of the overall coverage of the chapter and concluding remarks.

- **References**

Plagiarism and Citing

It is important to understand plagiarism and citing. Since most of the material in your book will be a product of research, meaning that it will be someone else's work, you should take extra care to avoid plagiarism and to cite wherever it is appropriate. The following abstracts are from Plagiarism.org, which provides details on plagiarism and how to avoid it:

What is Plagiarism?

Many people think of plagiarism as copying another's work, or borrowing someone else's original ideas. But terms like "copying" and "borrowing" can disguise the seriousness of the offense:

According to the Merriam-Webster Online Dictionary, to "plagiarize" means

1. to steal and pass off (the ideas or words of another) as one's own

2. to use (another's production) without crediting the source

3. to commit literary theft

4. to present as new and original an idea or product derived from an existing source.

In other words, plagiarism is an act of fraud. It involves both stealing someone else's work and lying about it afterward. Most cases of plagiarism can be avoided, however, by citing sources. Simply acknowledging that certain material has been borrowed, and providing your audience with the information necessary to find that source, is usually enough to prevent plagiarism.

What is citation?

A "citation" is the way you tell your readers that certain material in your work came from another source. It also gives your readers the information necessary to find that source again, including:

- information about the author
- the title of the work
- the name and location of the company that published your copy of the source
- the date your copy was published
- the page numbers of the material you are borrowing

Giving credit to the original author by citing sources is the only way to use other people's work without plagiarizing. But there are a number of other reasons to cite sources:

- Citations are extremely helpful to anyone who wants to find out more about your ideas and where they came from.

- Not all sources are good or right -- your own ideas may often be more accurate or interesting than those of your sources. Proper citation will keep you from taking the rap for someone else's bad ideas.

- Citing sources shows the amount of research you've done.

- Citing sources strengthens your work by lending outside support to your ideas.

Citing sources actually helps your reader distinguish your ideas from those of your sources. This will also emphasize the originality of your own work.

When to cite?

Whenever you borrow words or ideas, you need to acknowledge their source. You do not have to cite sources for facts that are not the result of unique individual research. Facts that are readily available from numerous sources and generally known to the public are considered "common knowledge," and are not protected by copyright laws. You can use these facts liberally without citing authors. If you are unsure whether or not a fact is common knowledge, you should probably cite your source just to be safe.

As a general rule of thumb, you can use the following table:

If you are using ...	Action
A Direct quote	Cite
Common knowledge (found in at least 3 sources)	No need to cite
Paraphrase or summary of ideas	Cite
Paraphrase of commonly known facts	No need to cite
Not common knowledge (less than 3 sources)	Cite
Quote or paraphrase of published research	Cite

More information on how to use material other than your own can be found in O'Reilly's Guide to authors at http://www.oreilly.com/oreilly/author/index.html.

CHAPTER 5

46 Revising and Editing Tips

Introduction

Good writers revise their work to ensure that the writing is clear and powerful. Most professional authors will tell you they revise a piece of writing a dozen times or more before it is published. Drafting is the stage in which a writer puts his plan into action while focusing on getting ideas down; mechanics and spelling are not of primary concern at this stage.

If you want someone else other than yourself to read your writing, you will want to make sure that your ideas are stated as clearly as possible. The process of getting to clarity is revision. Revision involves adding, deleting, moving or changing information to convey the message of the writing more effectively. Revision may take place at the word, sentence, and paragraph or whole-text level. Sometimes revision may even mean starting over.

After some revising your writing will say what you want it to say. Your ideas will be focused and all the needed details that support and enhance the main concept will have been included. Your information will be logically organized and you will have created an engaging lead and an effective conclusion. You will also have used the most powerful and precise words to convey the intended messages and created the needed images.

Next, it is time to clean up any errors in spelling and conventions before the writing is seen by an audience.

Many people tend to confuse or combine the processes of revision and editing, or neglect the revision component entirely. Even the terminology can be confusing. Some people consider editing to be the process of revising for meaning, while proofreading is the process of correcting surface errors. In the book business, "substantive editing" is the term used for major suggestions to the author; "copyediting" for the stage where minor errors and facts are checked before typesetting; and "proofing" for corrections just before the book is printed. Usually the substantive editor, copyeditor and proofreader are three different people.

Experienced writers tend to undertake both revision and editing at the same time, for example, deleting an unnecessary apostrophe at the same time as fleshing out a missing detail. However, for novice writers, it's a good idea to separate the two processes. After all, the more things a young writer must attend to, the less attention he is likely to pay to each one of them. Wait until all the content is in place before you focus on mechanical details.

For some people, editing is even more difficult than revising. Because we are trained to read for meaning, we sometimes read what makes sense rather than what is actually there. Reading aloud sometimes helps the reader focus on one word or sentence at a time. Starting at the end and reading backward helps the reader examine each word rather than the overall meaning of the text.

The Basics of Revising and Editing

    1. Get some distance! It is hard to revise or edit a manu-

script that you have just finished writing—it is still too familiar, and you tend to skip over many errors. Put the manuscript aside for a few hours, days, or weeks. Clear your head of what you have written so you can look at the manuscript fresh and see clearly, what is really on the pages.

2. Decide what medium lets you read most carefully. Some people like to work right at the computer, while others like to sit back with a printed copy that they can mark up as they read.

3. Try changing the look of your document - altering the size, spacing, color, or style of the text may trick your brain into thinking that it is seeing an unfamiliar document, and can help you get a different perspective on what you have written.

4. Find a quiet place to work. Don't try to do your revising or editing in front of the TV. Find a place where you can concentrate and avoid distractions.

5. Revise and edit in several short blocks of time, rather than all at once - otherwise, your concentration is likely to wane.

6. If you are short on time, you may wish to prioritize your revising and editing tasks to make sure that you will complete the most important ones.

Revising

7. When you revise look for places in your manuscript where you need to cut something out, places where you should add something, and places where you need to move or rearrange something. Revising doesn't mean fixing problems such as grammar and spelling. That's what's called "editing", and we'll get to that later.

Finding problems

8. First of all you have to put aside everything you know about the background of your book — what you intended, the real situation it might be based on — and react to what you have actually written.

9. Don't waste time by stopping to fix things. Read with a pen in your hand so that when you come to a point where something that doesn't quite feel right, put a squiggle in the margin beside it, then keep reading.

10. Trust your feelings. If you feel that there is something wrong—even if you don't know what it is—your readers will too.

11. The first time you read through each section, chapter, or even a paragraph, think only about these questions:

    - Have I repeated myself here or waffled on?

    - Is there something missing here?

    - Are parts of this in the wrong order?

Fixing problems

12. After having read your manuscript through, go back to each of the squiggles you made, and work out just why it didn't sound right.

    - If you repeated something, you need to cut.

    - If you have missed something, you need to add.

    - If parts are in the wrong order, you need to move things around.

13. If the problem is something else—spelling or grammar, for example—leave it for the moment. You will fix those later.

14. If you want to find problems before your readers do, you

have to try to read it the way they will. That means reading it straight through without stopping, to get a feeling for the manuscript as a whole. Read it aloud if you can—it will sound quite different and you'll hear where things should be changed.

What to look for in detail

15. Before you start making detailed revisions, you need to look at the following very important issues:

- **Content**
  - ○ Have you made your subject and your thesis on this subject clear to your readers?
  - ○ Are the claims you make accurate?
  - ○ Are your arguments complete?
  - ○ Are all of your claims consistent?
  - ○ Have you supported each point with adequate evidence?
  - ○ Is all of the information in your book relevant to the subject and/or your overall writing goal?

- **Overall Structure**
  - ○ Do your book and all its chapters have an appropriate introduction and conclusion?
  - ○ Is your thesis clearly stated in your introduction?
  - ○ Is it clear how each chapter is related to your thesis?
  - ○ Are the paragraphs/chapters arranged in a logical sequence?

- o Have you made clear transitions between paragraphs/chapters?

- **Structure within Paragraphs**

  - o Does each paragraph have a clear topic sentence?

  - o Does each paragraph stick to one main idea?

  - o Are there any extraneous or missing sentences in any of your paragraphs?

- **Clarity**

  - o Have you defined any important terms that might be unclear to your reader?

  - o Is the meaning of each sentence clear?

  - o Is it clear what each pronoun (he, she, it, they, which, who, this, etc.) refers to?

  - o Have you chosen the proper words to express your ideas? (Avoid using words you find in the thesaurus that aren't part of your normal vocabulary; you may misuse them.)

- **Style**

  - o Have you used an appropriate tone (formal, informal, persuasive, etc.)?

  - o Is your use of gendered language (masculine and feminine pronouns like "he" or "she," words like "fireman" that contain "man," and words that some people incorrectly assume apply to only one gender--for example, some people assume "nurse" must refer to a woman) appropriate?

  - o Have you varied the length and structure of your sentences?

- o Do you tend to use the passive voice too often?

- o Does your writing contain many unnecessary phrases like "there is," "there are," "due to the fact that," etc.?

- o Do you repeat a strong word (for example, a vivid main verb) unnecessarily?

- **Citations**
  - o Have you appropriately cited quotes, paraphrases, and ideas you got from sources?
  - o Are your citations in the correct format?

16. As you edit, you will usually make significant revisions to the content and wording of your book. Keep an eye out for patterns of error; knowing what kinds of problems you tend to have will be helpful. Once you have identified a pattern, you can develop techniques for spotting and correcting future instances of that pattern.

17. As you read through your draft, look for the necessary changes that will help your readers understand the given information better or be more convinced by your argument. Once you have identified the places that need fixing, you have to decide whether to cut, add or move.

- **What to Cut**:
  - o Padding. Too little information or argument taking up too much space;
  - o Waffle. Pompous or over-elaborate sentences with no real purpose;
  - o Repeated ideas or information.
  - o Irrelevant material. (even if it is brilliant or took you hours to write, it has to address the

main issue);

- o Words, sentences or even whole ideas. If your book tends to grow very big.

- **What to Add**:
  - o Information that you have assumed but not actually stated. (don't rely on the reader to fill the gaps)

  - o A step in your argument that you might have left out.

  - o Details or explanations that show how your ideas relate to the issue you are addressing.

  - o Connectors or pointers that smooth the flow between your ideas.

  - o The introduction and conclusion.

- **What to Move**:
  - o Information that's not in the most logical order.

  - o Information that is important but given to the reader at the wrong time (for example, background information that should go before the main argument).

  - o Steps in an argument that are not, in the most logical order (an argument has to build up step by step, with the evidence for each step, and then a final, convincing statement);

  - o Information that might be relevant or addressing the main issue, but interrupt the flow.

When Revising is "Too much"?

18. Do not throw away anything that you delete during the revision process. You might decide you were right earlier and you need to go back.

19. On a second reading, some of the problems appear to melt away. You have to remember, though, that most manuscripts don't get a second reading.

20. Don't worry about 'overworking' your manuscript until you have revised it at least three times.

21. Revising can actually be the best part of writing. You have already done the hard work—you have actually created a book out of thin air. You don't have to do that again. Now you can enjoy tinkering with it, adding here, cutting there—getting the whole thing as good as you can make it.

Editing

22. The next step is to edit your manuscript. You have come to the point where you have completed evaluating your manuscript for content and structure. Now, it is time to look at the individual sentences and words. What you are after is, to make your manuscript as reader-friendly as possible, by making the sentences flow in a clear and easy-to-read way.

23. You must also check for accepted ways of using English: use of appropriate grammar for your purposes, appropriate punctuation and spelling, and appropriate paragraphing.

Editing for Spelling

24. Spelling affects the way your reader perceives you and your message. Fortunately, you don't have to know how

to spell every word in the English (or any other) language. You have two great tools to help you spell correctly: Your computer spell checker and a dictionary.

25. Although the spell checker in your word processing software is a handy tool, you need to be careful when relying on it. Often, it will not recognize certain words, such as names, abbreviations, or terms that you have defined in your book, and it will tell you they are misspelled. In addition, some words that sound alike are spelled differently. If a word exists in the spell checker's dictionary, the spell checker will not catch that the word is misspelled in the context you are using it. For example, a spell checker will usually miss this misspelled word: "The ball broke my window pain." Although "pain" is a word, it's not spelled correctly here. It should be "pane". So use your head when making changes suggested by a spell checker.

26. Don't allow the spell checker to fix automatically the spelling in your book. You will have to go through every spell checker's suggestion to determine which words really are spelled incorrectly.

27. Use a dictionary as your backup.

Editing for Grammar

28. Like poor spelling, poor grammar can doom an otherwise very good book. It gives your reader a bad impression and takes away from your credibility.

29. The correct use of grammar is big subject, and it is strongly suggested that you get a specialized book. The following is just a quick checklist of some of the most common grammatical problems.

Use of Passive Voice

30. In most instances, put the verb in the active voice rather

than in the passive voice. Passive voice produces a sentence in which the subject receives an action. In contrast, active voice produces a sentence in which the subject performs an action. Passive voice often produces unclear, wordy sentences, whereas active voice produces generally clearer, more concise sentences.

31. To change a sentence from passive to active voice, determine who or what performs the action, and use that person or thing as the subject of the sentence.

Incorrect Punctuation of Two Independent Clauses

(An independent clause has a subject and a verb and can stand alone as a sentence.)

32. Good writers know that correct punctuation is important to writing clear sentences. If you misuse a mark of punctuation, you risk confusing your reader and appearing careless.

33. Writers often combine independent clauses in a single compound sentence to emphasize the relationship between ideas. The punctuation of compound sentences varies depending upon how you connect the clauses. The rules are:

- Separate independent clauses with a comma when using a coordinating conjunction (and, but, or, for, nor, so, yet).

- Separate independent clauses with a semi-colon when no coordinating conjunction is used.

- Separate independent clauses with a semi-colon when using a conjunctive adverb (e.g., however, therefore, thus, consequently, finally, nevertheless).

Wordiness

34. Concise writing is the key to clear communication.

Wordiness obscures your ideas and frustrates your reader.

35. Make your points as succinctly as possible, and move on. As Strunk and White, tell us in Elements of Style: "Vigorous writing is concise. A sentence should not contain unnecessary words; a paragraph should not contain unnecessary sentences.... This requires not that the writer makes all sentences short, or avoid all detail and treat subjects only in outline, but that every word tells."

36. Once you start searching for unnecessary words, you will find you can cut many without any loss of meaning. In fact, your writing will be crisper and more appealing. Remember: make "every word tells."

- **Strategies for eliminating wordiness**:
    - Use action verbs rather than forms of the verb to be (is, are, was, were).
    - Make the real subject the actual subject of the sentence; make the real verb the actual verb.

37. As a first step in reducing wordiness, locate instances of "this is", "there are", and "it is" at the beginning of your sentences, and ask yourself whether you can eliminate them.

Misuse of the Apostrophe

38. Use the apostrophe to indicate possession and to mark omitted letters in contractions. Writers often misuse apostrophes when forming plurals and possessives.

39. The basic rule is quite simple: use the apostrophe to indicate possession, not a plural. Yes, the exceptions to the rule may seem confusing: hers has no apostrophe, and it's is not possessive. Nevertheless, with a small amount of attention, you can learn the rules and the exceptions of

apostrophe use.

Misplaced and Dangling Modifiers

40. Misplaced and dangling modifiers create illogical, even comical, sentences. You will confuse your readers if you fail to connect modifiers (words that describe or limit other words) to the words they modify; be sure to place modifiers next to the words they modify. See the illogic in this example:

> *Walking back from the village, my wallet was lost.* (Does your wallet walk?)
>
> **Revised:**
>
> *Walking back from the village, I lost my wallet.* (Your wallet doesn't walk, but you do.)

41. A **misplaced modifier** is a word or phrase that due to its placement mistakenly refers to the wrong word. To correct a misplaced modifier, move it next to or near the word, it modifies.

42. **Limiting modifiers** (only, almost, nearly, just) are commonly misplaced. To avoid ambiguity, place them in front of the word they modify.

43. A **dangling modifier** is a (usually introductory) word or phrase that the writer intends to use as a modifier of a following word, but the following word is missing. The result is an illogical statement. To fix a dangling modifier, add the missing word and place the modifier next to it.

Pronoun Problems

44. Pronouns are useful as substitutes for nouns, but a poorly

chosen pronoun can obscure the meaning of a sentence. Common pronoun errors include:

- **Unclear Pronoun Reference** - A pronoun must refer to a specific noun (the antecedent). Ambiguous pronoun reference creates confusing sentences.

- **Vague Subject Pronoun** - Pronouns such as it, there, and this often make weak subjects.

Unclear Pronoun Reference Example:

> *You should spend time thinking about your arguments to make sure they are not superficial.* (Unclear antecedent: who or what are superficial?)
>
> *A key difference between banking crises of today and of yesterday is that they have greater global impact.* (Which crises have more impact?)

Vague Subject Pronoun Example:

> *Pope Gregory VII forced Emperor Henry IV to wait three days in the snow at Canossa before granting him an audience. It was a symbolic act.* (To what does "it" refer? Forcing the Emperor to wait? The waiting? The granting of the audience? The audience? The entire sentence?)

- **Agreement Error** - A pronoun must agree in gender and number with its antecedent. A common error is the use of the plural pronoun "they" to refer to a singular noun. It is often better to use a plural noun and pronoun than to use a singular noun and pronoun.

Mimicking Spoken Language

45. We do not always speak in complete sentences. Often, when we want our writing to sound natural and to flow smoothly, we write in a conversational style. This is OK when you are writing a dialogue and using appropriate punctuation to show that you are writing dialogue. Sometimes, professional writers will use this style of writing. However, you should avoid using conversational sentence fragments.

Capitalizing the Right Words

46. Here are some basic guidelines for capitalizing words.

- Capitalize the first word of a sentence: A sentence always begins with a capital letter.

- Capitalize I (including I'm, I've, I'd, and other contractions with I)

- Capitalize the first word in a quotation that is a complete sentence: If you are quoting only a phrase or part of a sentence, you don't need to capitalize the first word of the material you are quoting

- Capitalize the first and last words and all words that are not articles in the titles of movies, songs, works of art, and written materials: To Kill a Mockingbird, A Farewell to Arms, A Field Guide to Spiders and Scorpions of Texas

- Capitalize proper nouns and proper adjectives: Below is a list of what counts as a proper noun or a proper adjective:

  o People's names

  o Names of places

  o Names of businesses

- ○ Names of historical events
- ○ Things you find on a calendar (days, months, holidays)
- ○ Names of nationalities, races and religions
- ○ People's titles

CHAPTER 6

63 Layout & Design Tips

1. If you want your book to succeed, it must not look amateurish.

Book Size Basics

2. Varying the size of your book will vary your printing costs dramatically because printers buy paper in bulk and at certain sizes. Page size is contingent on the most economical fit for the paper that can also be accommodated on press. Listed below you will find the most common book sizes and the purpose that they are used for. You can always print at a size different from those listed but it will cost you extra.

   - 4 1/4" x 7" Mass Market
   - 5 1/2" x 8 1/2" Tradebook, Handbook or Fiction
   - 6" x 9" Handbook, Tradebook, or Fiction
   - 7" x 9" Manual, Textbook

- 7 1/2" x 9" Giftbook, Art Book, Manual

3. When choosing your book size, it is important to take into account the total number of pages in your book. You do not want a book too thin or too thick. If your book is originally written in a word document 8.5" x 11", it will likely double in pages when you size it down to 5.5"x 8.5". Therefore, 100 pages at 8.5"x 11" will likely be 200 pages at a 5.5"x 8.5" size. A 100 page book at 8.5"x 11" would look quite thin and unappealing but a 200 page book at a 5.5"x 8.5" size will likely make the reader feel that the book has substance.

Book Binding Basics

4. If you plan to publish your book using Print on Demand (POD) you must consider the available binding options.

5. If your book is a novel or collection of poems, **perfect binding** — like that used for mass-market paperbacks — is the most common choice. On the other hand, comics, magazines, and coloring books typically use **saddle-stitch binding** that lays flat. Technical manuals and how-to books that need to be open wide so pages can be easily flipped usually work best with **Wire** binding.

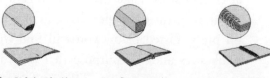

Saddle Stich Binding   Perfect Binding   Wire Binding

6. Choose the method of binding which provides the most usability required by the book's content and your target customers' needs. Look through your chosen genre to see what types of binding are used most often to help make your choice.

Book Layout Basics

7. Your next step will be to layout your book using your chosen book size. Before we move into the mechanics of book layout using MS Word or any other word processing software, you need to develop a clear idea about how you want your book to look. For example:

    - How much white space ("margin") will there be at the top, bottom, inside and outside of each page?

    - What type font? What size? How much spacing between lines of type?

    - Where will the page numbers appear? Does the title of the book and the author's name appear on the pages? If so, where?

    - What does a chapter opening look like?

    - How will the title page and other "front matter" and "back matter" pages be organized (copyright page, acknowledgments, dedication, possibly a blurb about the author, advance reviews, barcode, etc.)?

The Front Cover

8. Your book cover must perform several basic functions, quickly or you risk the words inside never being read. Here's what a good book cover does:

    - A good book cover design will convey - visually - the book's message.

    - The book cover should generate feelings of excitement and anticipation, making the potential reader eager to dig in to discover more.

    - A truly good book cover will "SELL" the book on its own.

9. Check out the people in a bookstore and watch how they browse. 99.9% of the time, they will let their eyes wander over the books on display, sometimes for several minutes before picking up a book. When they do pick one up, they look at the front cover, flip over to the back, and if they're still interested might take a sneak peek at the first page or two inside. All this happens in seconds - that's how long you have to attract a reader, retailer, or reviewer. The book cover design will have the biggest impact on whether people pick up your book instead of someone else's.

10. Consumers buy with their eyes, and they will instinctively look for something that appears to be quality. Book covers that aren't as well-designed as others are, lose value.

11. Traditionally, writers tend to put all their efforts into writing the book and ignore the cover. After having spent massive amounts of time writing the content of their books, it almost seems like a trivial task for a writer to wrap it with a cover. Unfortunately, not enough care and planning will lead to sloppy, poor covers. Take some time; don't rush to go to print.

12. Whether a book cover is successful or not depends on the book genre and the target audience. You have to appeal to your audience. If your cover doesn't appeal to your audience and offer some real incentive, your audience doesn't exist. Find out what you target audience likes and dislikes. Some market research will help you in that task.

13. Practice makes perfect. The cover is such an important sales piece for your book that it is worth spending your time and, perhaps, money to get it right. A good way of doing that is to make up some test covers sheets on your computer. Print these out and wrap them around any

book to see how they look.

14. Do not use more than two types of fonts in your front cover.

15. The two most important parts of the front cover are the title and subtitle. The subtitle should be as descriptive as possible but not too wordy. Add your name and you have the essential pieces of text for your cover.

16. Make sure any graphics on the cover are crisp, clean, and preferably related to the book's subject; otherwise make them neutral i.e. abstract patterns, solid colors, etc. If you like to play around with colors have a look in AP-PENDIX E – Color and Book Cover Design: A Reference Chart for information regarding the psychological impact of colors.

17. Make sure any artwork that will serve, as background is not too distracting so it will not reduce the impact of the title. You can incorporate your title and subtitle into the artwork as long as they remain legible.

18. Do not pick artwork that has cryptic meanings, as your readers will not probably understand it.

19. **Make sure you have license to use artwork found from the internet.**

20. If you want your book cover to look original, you should not use cover art software because they are mostly based on templates, which eventually will be or have been used by others. Download a trial version of Adobe Photoshop or other equivalent graphics software and design your book cover from scratch. If you have never used a graphics software before type "photoshop tutorials" in Google and you will find all the information you will ever need. When your book starts selling, use some of the profits to buy the program.

21. Cover artwork over the years has advanced greatly due to the powerful, relatively available graphics software. Most writers are not graphic artists. If you are one of them find someone who is. It's worth the effort and the money.

22. Finally, visit bookstores and book websites and look at other books in the same category as your book and check what covers styles are used. Don't be afraid to ask for advice from publishers and authors alike in writing or publishing forums. They are usually willing to help.

The Back Cover

23. Even if your book will be sold solely as a download, it still needs a back cover. In fact, you must give to your back cover the same attention as your front cover. Many authors loose sales because of a bad back cover or even worse no back cover at all.

24. Back cover copy can either walk your book right up to the cash register or march it back to the shelves. Back cover copy should be an open invitation to the reader to cross the threshold of a book. It should be provocative and engaging enough to hook a reader's interest.

25. Back cover copy should provide a small preview of what's inside so that a reader could get an idea of what to expect. Good back cover copy should include significant details that may incidentally appeal to your audience and make the difference between sealing the deal and sending your book back to sit on the shelf.

26. Back cover copy should have less than 70 words, for a 6" by 9" book. Use emotional words; benefits, not features; and testimonials to capture your readers' attention and to keep your message focused. Make every word count. For self-help books use bullets with specific benefits, and enough of the right kind of testimonials to sell your book

in 8 seconds. Visit local and online bookstores to search for ideas.

27. Write only a one or two-line bio on the back cover.

28. Include a "Hot Headline" – not the book title -, which describes your best benefit and should compel your reader to buy. Notice the headlines in your newspaper. Visit your bookstore and notice other best selling authors' headlines.

    - "What's So Tough About Writing?" by Richard Lederer, author of The Write Way;

    - "Imagine Being an Author", in Dan Poynter's Writing Nonfiction; or

    - "To Age is Natural...To Grow Old is Not!" heads Rico Caveglia's "Ageless Living" back cover.

29. Your book's back cover should also include:

    - **Category** - Visit a bookstore (online or not) and check the available categories on the books and the shelves. Listing the category on the back cover of your book will ensure your book will be easy to find because it will be placed in the right position.

    - **A sale closer in bold type** - Ask the book-browser to buy the book. Use something like "This book has enabled thousands to . . . and it will show you the way too."

    - **Price** - Bookstores like to show the price on the book. However, price is a big turn-off to potential buyers so place it at the end of the sales copy. Never locate the price at the top of the back cover. If it's a hardcover book, place the price at the top of the front flap.

    - **Bar code with International Standard Book**

Number (ISBN) - The bar code on a book identifies the ISBN, which in turn identifies the publisher, title, author and edition (hardcover, etc.).

Book Back Cover Example

Book: Digital Lighting & Rendering

Testimonials

Publisher Information

ISBN & Price

Book Shelf Category

Benefits Description

Author Bio

Between The Covers

30. In traditional book publishing the parts (or sections) of a

book, its layout and reading order follow relatively strict conventions. All books are divided into 3 main parts:

- **Front Matter** - Front Matter refers to all the material that appears at the front of the book, before you reach the actual body content. This includes the Title Page, Table of Contents, List of Figures/Illustrations, Preface, Forward, Dedication, and Acknowledgement.

- **Main Body** - This is the main portion part of the book where the main text, story or description can be found. In longer books and manuals, the body is often sub-divided into chapters or sections.

- **End of the Book Components (Back Matter)** - These refer to all the material usually found at the end of the book. Depending on the type of the book, they might include Appendices, Bibliography, Glossary and an Index.

Title Page

31. The title page would at least have the title of the book and the name of the author and illustrator. Depending on the type of your book, you may include some additional information. Technical or software manuals may include more information on the specific products covered, safety notices, and warranties. Other data that could be included in the title page are:

- Publisher Name and Address
- Copyright information
- ISBN
- Library of Congress number
- Edition Notice
- Date of publication

- Number of printings
- Disclaimers
- Warranties
- Safety Notices

Table of Contents

32. A table of contents may be very simple (plain listing of all the main chapter titles and the page they start) or it may contain multi-level listings with sub-chapters and descriptions.

List of Figures / Illustrations

33. If you are writing a technical book, it is a good idea to include a separate table of contents for the illustrations, photos, and graphs providing the name or source of the illustration, a title or description of the illustration, and the page number.

Preface

34. The purpose of the preface is to get the reader's attention by briefly describing the contents, purpose of the book, and explaining whom the book targets.

Foreword

35. Often written by an acknowledged expert in the field or genre covered by the book, the foreword is something of a testimonial for the author or the book itself.

Dedication

36. The dedication section is a separate page that briefly names one or more persons of special significance to the author, often a loved one or someone else the author holds in high esteem.

Acknowledgment

37. The acknowledgment page is where the author acknowledges the contributions of organizations and individuals who he or she feels helped with the book.

Appendix (Back Matter)

38. An Appendix is a place at the end of the book where you can put the material that doesn't fit within the body of the book.

Bibliography (Back Matter)

39. The bibliography is a list of resources related to the subject of the book. The bibliography may list other books, magazines or specific articles, and Web sites.

Glossary (Back Matter)

40. The glossary, like a dictionary, lists acronyms, words, and phrases relevant to the subject of the book along with their definition. The glossary is essential if you are writing a technical book or if your book contains many terms that might be unknown to most people.

Index

41. The Index is an alphabetical list of all the sub-topics and ideas covered in the body of the book, along with the page number(s) where they appear in the book.

Common Elements

42. Common Elements are pieces of data, which appear throughout the whole book providing the reader with a sense of direction within the book. Such elements are:

    - **Header / Footer** - Repeating text - often the title of the book or the specific chapter within the book - that appears at the top (header) or bottom (footer) of each page or every other page in a book design. Headers and footers are also the place where page numbers appear.

- **Page Numbers** - Page numbers can appear at the top, bottom, or sides of pages although the bottom of the page is the most common place. Usually, Roman numerals (i, ii, iii ...) are sometimes used for the front matter and Arabic page numbering (1, 2, 3 ...) starts with the first chapter. Material at the end of the book, such as an appendix, may have a separate numbering system such as A-1, A-2, etc. for Appendix A.

Fonts

43. There is only one rule in selecting fonts for your book's main body. **The text must be legible and easy to read.**

44. Body text should be between 10 and 12 point, with 11 point best for printing to 300 dot-per inch printers. Use the same typeface, type size, and leading (the white space between the lines) for all body copy.

45. Use enough leading. Always add at least 1 or 2 points to the type face.

46. Don't make your lines too short or too long. Optimum size is between 30 and 70 characters.

47. Make paragraph beginnings clear.

48. Use only one space after a period.

49. Don't justify text unless you have to.

50. Don't underline anything.

51. Use italics instead of underlines.

52. Don't set long blocks of text in italics, bold, or all caps because they are hard to read.

53. Leave more space above headlines and subheads than below them, and avoid setting them in all caps. Use subheads liberally to help readers find what they are looking for.

How to Put It All Together Professionally!

54. Convention dictates that a book has two pages, the left (L) and the right (R). This is important because certain pieces of information should be displayed on either the right (R) or the left (L) page.

55. The first page the reader usually sees upon opening a book will be the right-hand half-title page. It usually displays only the book's title, not the author name, subtitle, or other parts of a full title page (see below). The inside of the front cover is left blank.

56. It is very common to leave the reverse of the half-title page (the following left-hand page) blank. However, a number of items could appear on this page: a list of your previous works or other titles if your book is part of a series. If none of those exists, this is where a dedication could be placed.

57. The title page always appears on the right (R) and contains:

   - Full title, including the subtitle if one exists;

   - Name of the author or names of authors if the book is collaboration;

   - Names of contributors, such as editors, illustrators, and translators; and

   - Name of the publisher and the publisher's logo.

58. You may choose to place the table of contents on the right-hand page opposite the copyright page (also called

imprint page), or you may instead place the dedication. It is more important to remember that convention states that half title, title, foreword, contents, and preface should be on right-hand pages, and should appear in the same order as mentioned.

59. Pages following the preface might include an introduction, list of illustrations, list of acknowledgements, and a dedication if this hasn't been shown on the half-title left-hand page.

60. Because of this pagination, you will end up with blank pages appearing in the front matter. Blank pages are included in the pagination flow, but neither the number nor the header/footer should be displayed on these pages.

Covers

LOCATION	PAGE NAME	CONTENT
Front of the Book	Front Cover	Graphic, book title, subtitle (if any), author name(s).
Inside Front Cover		Usually blank; optional to include ISBN or UPC (Universal Product Code) numbers and bar codes.
Vertical Spine	Spine	Title, Author(s), Publisher logo (if available).
Inside Back Cover		BLANK
Back of the Book	Back Cover	• Brief description of book's content. • Author photo & qualifications (both optional, but highly recommended). • Book review/promotional

		quotes (definitely include if available). • ISBN + bar code (will be printed if available; be sure to leave sufficient white space).

Front Matter

LOCATION	PAGE NAME	CONTENT
1st R page after inside front cover.	OPTIONAL Promo Page OR blank	If used as Promo, include testimonials, reviews, or endorsements for the book; may also list author's other books Otherwise, leave BLANK.
1st L page		BLANK
2nd R page	Half Title Page	Contains only the title of the book, not author name(s) or subtitle (if any).
L page facing full title page.		BLANK
R page	Full Title Page	Display full title, subtitle (if any), & name of the author(s), editor or compiler of collection, photos, etc. (if any).
L page (Reverse of the Title Page contains the copyright	Copyright Page	Notice of Copyright consists of these parts: "Copyright 200X by [Author(s) Name]. All rights reserved. No part of this book

notice, printing history, the Library of Congress Catalog number, ISBN, publisher, name/address, & any additional copyright information.)		may be used or reproduced in any manner whatsoever without written permission, except in the case of brief quotations embodied in critical articles or reviews. Published 200X by [Publisher's Name] ISBN X-XXX-XXXXX-X" NOTE: When text & photographs (or other content) have different copyright owners, list them individually: "Text copyright 200X by [Author(s) Name] Photographs copyright 200X by [Photographer(s) Name]"
R page	Dedication Page	Short statement thanking an individual or group of individuals for their help or support.
L page (Reverse of the Dedication Page)		BLANK
R page	Acknowledgements	OPTIONAL. List of everyone who helped the author produce the book, otherwise SKIP AHEAD TO TABLE OF CONTENTS
L page (Reverse of Acknowledgements Page)		Not needed if you skipped the Acknowledgements. Otherwise BLANK

R page	Table of Contents (TOC)	Lists the book's contents, arranged by chapter. Can also break down by chapter section and/or subsection.
L page	TOC continued if needed. Otherwise BLANK	If TOC covers more than one pages, continue using consecutive L and R pages. If the TOC ends on a L page, start Chapter 1 on the next R page. If it ends on a R page, insert a BLANK L page, then start Chapter 1 on next R page
R page (Any of the described sections, if included, should start on a R page.)	OPTIONAL Foreword Preface Introduction List of Abbreviations List of Illustrations Disclaimers	ALL ARE OPTIONAL: **Foreword:** Testimonial or introduction by someone other than the author. **Preface:** Explanation of the origins & history of the book written by the book's author(s). **Introduction:** Short summary or explanation of the book. **List of Abbreviations:** List of the abbreviations contained in the book. **List of Illustrations:** List of all illustrations, figures or diagrams, with page numbers where they can be found in the book **Disclaimers:** Short conditional statement about the use of the book. Included to provide a small amount of legal protection to the author.

Main Body

LOCATION	PAGE NAME	CONTENT
R page	Chapter One Can be spelled out or displayed in numerals	Name of the chapter & body text of chapter. Chapter continues in consecutive L and R pages.
L or R page	Chapters	Convention dictates that each new Chapter starts on an R page, even if that means the preceding L page is BLANK. However, it is perfectly acceptable to continue L/R pagination throughout the remaining body text of your book without forcing a R page start for each new chapter. The primary reason for not forcing R page starts for each new chapter is to save paper.

End of the Book (Back Matter)

LOCATION	PAGE NAME	CONTENT
R page	OPTIONAL End Notes Appendix	**End Notes:** Additional information about a statement made in the text & usually referenced by a number. **Appendix:** Collection of important information & other

		resources.
R page	OPTIONAL Glossary Bibliography	**Glossary:** List of terms found in the book & their definitions. **Bibliography:** List of books, articles & other resources the author used in writing the book.
R page	OPTIONAL Works Cited Index Author Bio	**Works Cited:** List of books, articles & other resources the author cited in the text of the book. **Index:** List of key words & associated page numbers designed to help the reader find important information inside the book. The Index should not list chapters, but rather terms & concepts found within chapters. Indexing is a combination of skill & intuition. Usually the last section in a book. **Author Bio:** Short author biography (possibly including photo) is usually included in all books other than a mass-market paperback Do not include in back matter if also displayed on back cover.

Common Design and Layout Mistakes

61. Design pre-sells the importance of your words. Your readers will start evaluating your publication before they actually start reading it. In many cases, readers will begin judging the value of your publication by its appearance.

62. Quality design will differentiate your book from the competition and will build trust in your name, which will make it easier for you to sell your future titles.

63. Here are the most common design mistakes:

    • **Too much color** - Too much use of Color can send the wrong message. Readers are aware that color is often used to camouflage lack of content. In addition, bright colors can create distractions or make text hard to read. **You should always use the minimum amount of color needed to brighten your pages or convey your message.**

    • **Missing page numbers** - Readers depend on page numbers to track their progress through a publication. Readers also rely on page numbers to refer back to previously read information.

    • **Boring similarity** - Your publication should convey to your readers that it is something new or different. You can achieve that with your book cover, which should not resemble the covers of hundreds of other books the readers have encountered. In most cases, the interior pages use the same typeface, type size, line spacing, and text alignment, regardless of who published the book, because the writers used the built-in templates in Microsoft Word – the most popular word processing software.

    • **Narrow Margins.** Narrow margins can cause two

problems:

- ○ Long lines of text which make the book harder to read, and

- ○ Lack of white space so the reader doesn't have a resting spot for his/her eyes and the text is not properly emphasized.

- **Inappropriate typeface** - There are three main classifications of type: decorative, serif, and sans serif:

  - ○ Decorative typefaces - like Impact or Broadway - are heavily stylized and great for attracting attention or projecting an atmosphere or image. They should be used only where image is more important than readability.

Serif Fonts

  - ○ Serif typefaces - like Times New Roman or Garamond—are ideal for reading especially printed material. The finishing strokes each character help lead the reader's eyes from letter to letter.

Sans Serif Fonts

  - ○ Sans serif typefaces - like Arial or Verdana - are very legible. They have a clean and simple design that makes text easy to read on screen or from a distance, like in road signs.

- **Too large or too small type** - Too small type does not allow all the details to be seen, thus making the text harder to read. Too large type does not allow enough space for words in each line, which, again, makes the text harder to read. Keep in mind that comfortable reading requires about 40 to 45 characters per line.

- **Improper line and paragraph spacing** - Correct

line spacing - called leading - depends on typeface, type size and line length. White space between lines the reader's eyes to move from one word to the next within the same line. Long lines, sans serif typefaces and large type size require more white space between the lines. Correct paragraph spacing is equally important. New paragraphs should be separated by noticeably more space than line spacing within paragraphs, but not too much space so that each paragraph gets isolated. Paragraph spacing should be equal to one and one half (1½) line spacing.

CHAPTER 7

16 Pricing Tips

A Few Definitions...

Price represents the exchange value of a product among other potential purchases. Pricing a product – in our case a book - is an art and an ever challenging task. Price is perhaps the most important of the four P's of marketing (Product, Price, Place, Promotion), since it is the only one that generates revenue.

Value is the ratio of perceived benefits to price. It indicates that a book has the right type and the right amount of benefits that are expected from a book at that specific price. In other words, value determines if the utility gained from the exchange is worth the buying power (money) that must be sacrificed.

Utility is an attribute that has the potential to satisfy wants. In order to be successful you must understand the value consumers derive from the product and use this as a basis for pricing it.

The Purpose of the Price

The book's price must cover the costs of production, design, distribution and promotion of the book and at the same time allow for profit.

Pricing a book correctly is difficult and must reflect the supply and demand relationship. Pricing a book too high or too low could mean a loss of sales. Pricing should take into account the following factors:

- Fixed and variable costs
- Competition
- Your objectives
- Proposed positioning strategies
- Target group and its willingness to pay.

The 3 C's of Effective Pricing

Cost – This includes the cost of your own work, the cost of doing research, the cost of acquired permissions to reprint, the cost for supplies and other needed materials, the cost for publishing the book, the cost for advertising and promotion, the cost of your website ...you get the idea! Do not leave anything out!

Competition – Do a lot of research, determine how others are pricing their books with similar topics, and try to find out how well they are performing. If you cannot find any performance data, ask your friends and family if they would buy your competitors' books at their asking prices, provided of course that they need the information. Then decide where you want to go against your competition.

Customers - Look at what your target market will bear. This has nothing to do with your competition's prices. Your market is your customers, the people you want to sell to. The maximum price that they are willing to pay is what this market will bear. This is the one of the most important considerations when setting your prices.

How to Price Your Book

1. Use **Competitive Pricing**. The concept behind this frequently used pricing strategy is to match the price established by an industry leader for a particular subject area. Since price difference is minimized with this strategy,

you will focus your efforts on other ways to attract new customers. Some examples of what you might do in order to obtain new customers include producing high-quality products, providing superior customer service, and/or engaging in creative marketing. Competitive pricing is employed when you wish to concentrate your competitive efforts on marketing variables other than price. Research has shown that more than two-thirds use the competitive pricing approach. According to Peter Drucker, "The only sound way to price is to start out with what the market is willing to pay…and design to that price."

2. Use **Prestige Pricing**. Another alternative is to promote, maintain, and enhance the image of your book through the use prestige pricing, which involves pricing it high enough, thus limiting its availability to the higher-end consumer. This limited availability enhances the book's image, causing it to be viewed as prestigious. Although you might expect limited sales, this is not a problem because a profit is still possible due to the higher markup on each item.

3. Use **Profitability Pricing**. The idea behind profitability pricing is to maximize profit. The basic formula for this strategy is that Profits equal Revenue minus Expenses ($P = R - E$). Revenue is determined by the book's selling price and the number of units sold. You must be careful not to increase the price too much, or the quantity sold will be reduced and total profits may be lower than desired. Therefore, you should always monitor the price of your book in order to make sure it is competitive while at the same time providing for an acceptable profit margin.

4. Use **Volume Pricing**. You can use volume pricing when you are looking to maximize sales while staying within

predetermined profit margins. The principle behind volume pricing is to price the product lower than normal and expect to profit from a higher sales volume. Volume pricing can be beneficial because the products are being purchased on a large scale, and large-scale product distribution helps to reinforce your name and increases customer loyalty.

How to Enter the Market

5. Use a **skimming pricing policy**, which involves setting prices relatively higher than other similar books and then gradually lowering prices. The skimming price is the highest possible price that buyers are willing to pay (skim the cream off the top -- skim the innovators). This market segment is more interested in quality, status, uniqueness, etc. This policy is effective in situations where your book has a substantial lead over competition. The book's quality and image must support its higher price, and enough buyers must be willing to buy the book at that price. Competitors should not be able to enter the market easily and undercut the high price. Skimming generates a high initial cash flow. Consumer demand must be inelastic.

6. Alternatively, you can use a **penetration pricing policy**, which involves setting prices lower than other similar books in hope to secure wide market acceptance, which will allow you to raise your prices later. Use this policy when you expect competition and you know that the low price will help keep out the competition or if your target market is highly price sensitive. Penetration is appropriate when demand is elastic.

7. You may also use **Psychological Pricing**, to enhance the pricing strategy of your choice. The concept of psychological pricing is that certain prices are more appealing

than others are. Examples of psychological pricing are:

- Reference Pricing, involving easy to remember prices which can also be used for reference,

- Image or Prestige Pricing is used as a measure of quality.

- Odd pricing is the practice of choosing such prices as $19.95, $.99, or $99.99, which emphasize low prices by attracting the buyer's attention to the first digit.

How to Maximize Sales

8. **Coupons** - You may have noticed that almost all companies offer product coupons and that can only mean one thing: coupons have numerous advantages. You can use coupons for many reasons: to introduce a new product, to enhance market share, to increase sales on a mature product, or revive an old product. Coupons can be used to generate new customers by getting customers to buy and try a product—in the hope that these trial purchases will result in repeat sales.

9. **Prepayment** - Prepayment, as a method for increasing in book sales can be used in the form of gift certificates. This way, consumers are encouraged to buy from you rather than from other sellers.

10. **Seasonal Pricing** - You can also adjust the price of your book based on seasonal demands. Seasonal pricing will help move books when they are least saleable. An advantage of seasonal pricing is that the price for a book is set high during periods of high demand and lowered as seasonal demand drops off.

11. **Volume Discounts** - This is a very common method where you offer discounts for large volume orders. The

idea behind this is simple—if a customer purchases a large volume of a product, the product is offered at a lower price. This tactic allows larger quantity sales at an acceptable profit margin. Volume pricing is also useful for building customer loyalty.

Pricing Guidelines

If all the above sound too confusing or you just don't want to get into that much detail right now, there are a few guidelines you can follow to price your book correctly.

12. As a rule of thumb, a price under $20 will make your book easier to sell. Most people spend $20 without thinking twice. Books priced between $20 and $50, are relatively easy to sell. Once you go above $50, it becomes very difficult to sell your book. Books in that price range are usually specialized and they offer some unique information, like manuals and educational courses.

13. The recommended startup price for a book is $19.97. You can increase that price later.

14. Sometimes a lower price may actually be more profitable. A lower price will probably generate more sales. For example, suppose you get two sales out of every 100 visitors at $19.97. That means that you have generated revenue of $39.94. If you raise the price to $29.97 will be great, but only of you can keep the 2% conversion rate (2 sales out of every 100 visitors). If your visitors aren't willing to pay this price tag, you will probably drop to 1% conversion rate, thus making only $29.97 out of every 100 visitors.

15. If you offer a money back guarantee – which is something you should very carefully consider - you will get fewer refund requests with a lower price. This is because people will not spend the time to get their money back

on lower priced items.

16. The strategy that will help you determine the price is called split-testing. Many free scripts will show different versions of your website based on time, geographic location, and number of visits. In this case, the only difference would be the price. Let your website run like this for a while and you will find out which price will generate more sales and more revenue. Remember that for accurate results, the two versions of your website must be identical and their only difference must be the price of your book.

Summary

Price is an important component of the four P's of marketing because it generates revenue. Several factors need to be examined when setting a product price. Frequently reviewed factors include pricing objectives, pricing strategies, and options for increasing sales, since all of these factors contribute to the price established for a product.

CHAPTER 8

10 Copyright & ISBN Tips

What is Copyright?

Copyright is a form of protection provided by the laws of the United States to the authors of "original works of authorship," including literary, dramatic, musical, artistic, and certain other intellectual works. This protection is available to both published and unpublished works.

We will be focusing on literary works, where books belong. Literary works include non-dramatic textual works with or without illustrations. They may be published or unpublished. Computer programs and databases also are considered literary works. Plays, dramas, and screenplays are not in the literary works category, since they belong to "Performing Arts".

Examples of literary works are:

- advertising copy
- automated databases

- bound or loose-leaf volumes
- brochures
- catalogs
- compilations of data or other literary subject matter
- computer programs
- contributions to collective works
- directories
- dissertations
- fiction
- games
- manuscripts
- nonfiction
- online works
- pamphlets
- poetry
- reference works
- reports
- secure tests
- single pages of text
- speeches
- textbooks
- theses
- tracts

The Copyright Act generally gives the owner of copyright the exclusive right to do and to authorize others to do the following:

- To reproduce the work in copies or phonorecords;

- To prepare derivative works based upon the work;

- To distribute copies or phonorecords of the work to the public by sale or other transfer of ownership, or by rental, lease, or lending;

- To perform the work publicly, in the case of literary, musical, dramatic, and choreographic works, pantomimes, and motion pictures and other audiovisual works;

- To display the work publicly, in the case of literary, musical, dramatic, and choreographic works, pantomimes, and pictorial, graphic, or sculptural works, including the individual images of a motion picture or other audiovisual work; and

- In the case of sound recordings, to perform the work publicly by means of a digital audio transmission.

Why Should You Copyright Your Book?

1. Copyright ensures certain minimum safeguards of the rights of authors over their creations, thereby protecting and rewarding creativity. Obtaining a United States copyright is basically an affordable insurance policy to protect your book while at the same time providing certain important advantages:

    - With Copyright Registration, you establish a public record of your work.

    - You will be able to sue anyone who has illegally used your work in any way, for copyright infringement.

    - You will be able receive statutory damages or attorneys fees in case of copyright infringement in an

unpublished book. The same holds true for published books, unless the registration is made within
three months after the first publication.

2. If you register your book within five years from its creation, it is considered "prima facie" evidence in court.
Prima facie evidence means that if you ever went to
court, the registration of your copyright would be sufficient evidence of your ownership of the copyrighted material. The only way for another party to win would be
for them to present evidence showing that:

- They had a pre-existing copyright claim to the
work.

- You permitted them to use your work.

- You didn't actually create the work.

- You stole it from them.

3. U.S. Copyright Registrations are recognized by the
courts in 167 countries!

4. The remedies available for infringement are broad. A
court can enjoin an infringer from continuing his infringement. The court can also order that all infringing
materials be seized. As for monetary damages, the injured
party can choose to receive either his actual damages or
profits made by the infringer or statutory damages,
which can be as high as $150,000.

Steps to Copyrighting Literary Works

5. Follow these steps to register your book, manuscript, online work, poetry, or other text:

- **Step 1** - Make sure your work is a literary work.
Literary works may be published or unpublished
and include non-dramatic textual works with or

without illustrations. Computer programs and databases also are considered literary works.

- **Step 2** - Put into one envelope or package a completed application Form, as follows:

  o A "Form TX" for registration of published or unpublished, non-dramatic, literary works, excluding periodicals or serial issues. This class includes a wide variety of works: fiction, nonfiction, poetry, textbooks, reference works, directories, catalogs, advertising copy, compilations of information, and computer programs.

  o A "Short Form TX", if (1) You are the only author and copyright owner of the work, and (2) The work was not made for hire, and (3) The work is completely new (does not contain a substantial amount of material that has been previously published or registered or is in the public domain).

  o A Communication Form "CON", if needed.

  o A $45 payment to "Register of Copyrights."

  o Nonreturnable copy(ies) of the material to be registered.

- **Step 3** - Send the package to:

  Library of Congress

  Copyright Office

  101 Independence Avenue, S.E.

  Washington, D.C. 20559-6000

Your registration becomes effective on the day that the Copyright

Office receives your application, payment, and copy(ies) in acceptable form. If your submission is in order, you will receive a certificate of registration in approximately 4 months.

> **Notice:**
>
> Please be aware that when you register your claim to a copyright in a work with the U.S. Copyright Office, you are making a public record. All the information you provide on your copyright registration is available to the public and will be available on the Internet.
>
> You will find all the above forms and detailed instructions at this address:
>
> http://www.copyright.gov/register/literary.html

Why Do You Need An ISBN?

The ISBN system was established in 1968 as a standard identification system. ISBN stands for "International Standard Book Number" and it is used to supply information about the publisher and edition details of a book. Each number is unique to that edition, i.e.: a hardcover, CD, or eBook format of the same title would each have their own unique number.

6. Today all book databases use the ISBN system. There is no legal requirement for a book to have an ISBN and registration conveys no form of legal or copyright protection, but if you wish to sell your publication through major bookselling chains, or internet booksellers, they will require you to have an ISBN. Bookstores will not order a book without an ISBN... mostly because they can't. Without an ISBN, there's no number for them to look up.

7. Likewise, if you want people to be able to find your book you must have an ISBN. Without this number, your book will not be recognized in the book databases and this would undoubtedly hurt your sales.

In the past ISBN numbers were 10 digits long but a new global standard, using 13 digits, has now been introduced. Under the new system which started on 1 January 2007, the 13 digits are always divided into five parts, separated by spaces or hyphens. The four parts following the prefix element can be of varying length and are as shown below.

- Prefix Element: For the foreseeable future this will be either 978 or 979.

- Registration Group Element: Identifies a national, geographic or language grouping of Publishers. It tells you where in the world the Publisher is based (not the language of the book).

- Registrant (Publisher) Element: Identifies a specific publisher or imprint.

- Publication Element: Identifies a specific edition of a specific title in a specific format.

- Check Digit: This is always and only the final digit which mathematically validates the rest of the number. It is calculated using a Modulus 10 system with alternate weights of 1 and 3.

How to Get an ISBN

8. Before you get an ISBN, you must make an important decision. Will you use your own ISBN or not? The better and most costly answer is to use your own ISBN, especially if you plan to write more books in the future.

9. You must be a publisher to be able to get an ISBN. As a publisher, you can have your own ISBN assigned to all of your books, as well as books written by other people. All you really need is a name for your publishing company and a P.O. Box. For $225, you can purchase 10 ISBNs and you are on your way. **Once you own your own ISBN, you are no longer a "self-publisher". You are a "publisher".**

10. You may ask yourself why go through all the trouble to become a publisher just so you can buy your own ISBN. Because, once you own the ISBN, it remains the same for the life of the book. You can change whatever you

wish (printers, distributors, wholesalers, retailers) but the book remains yours. If, ten years from now, someone orders a copy of your book, you, as the publisher, will get the order. If you don't own the number, the person who does will get the order. This is the main issue with certain Print on Demand (POD) companies who let you use one of their numbers, but you do not own it. The orders for that book (ISBN) will always go to that publisher. If you change publishers, the ISBN does not go with you; it remains theirs. You will need to start all over with your marketing efforts under your new ISBN number. You should consider using this option if you are on a small budget or do not plan to write any more books.

Once you have the experience of publishing your own book, you can help other writers be published—through your company, using one of your ISBNs.

TIP:

For more information on ISBN and application forms visit http://www.isbn.org.

CHAPTER 9

10 Print On Demand Tips

What Is Print On Demand (POD)?

According to WikiPedia, Print on demand (POD), sometimes mistakenly referred to as publish on demand, is a printing technology employed by publishers, in which new copies of a book (or other document) are not printed until after an order for them has been received.

1. Electronic books are great, but they have not yet reached mass acceptance by the consumer or reviewers. In the meantime, POD can help you get your book to readers in a format they are familiar with.

The costs and risks associated with the launch of every new book are closely related to the lifecycle of the book. The lifecycle of the book, as Voytko describes is like a bell curve: at the beginning of the bell curve, sales are typically slow as marketing efforts and reviews build demand. Once demand has increased, sales increase and eventually reach a plateau. From the plateau, sales decrease until the book goes out-of-print.

2. POD is very useful for minimizing costs and risks since this method helps to free publishers from the process of doing a traditional print run of several thousand books at a time.

For the first printing, books are usually produced in large enough quantities to justify traditional offset printing. After printing and binding the books are stored in warehouses or shipped to distributors. Publishers accept a great deal of risk when they commit to the length of press runs for first editions based on their estimates of potential sales. If book sales fail to ramp up as projected, the publisher faces returns, which must be warehoused, sold to discounters, or destroyed. If the sales ramp up more quickly than projected, the publisher may decide to do a second printing, which entails even more risk.

When demand slackens and a book goes out-of-print, it may not be because there are no customers or back orders for the book, but instead it may be too expensive to print a quantity of books using an offset press. Even if there are customers and back orders for a book, the number must be large enough to justify offset printing. This is where books printed on demand using digital printers can extend the lifecycle of a book indefinitely.

3. POD technology provides a cost effective method to print small quantities of books. Authors and publishers may enjoy the following benefits:

- Publishers do not have to estimate how many books to print; they can print the books as orders come in.

- There is no need for warehousing and all the associated costs.

Once the content is written, it can be converted into a format, such as PDF, PostScript, or TIFF files that can be stored electronically for printing. IBM provides the following description about the benefits of print on demand: *"For books nearly or completely out of print, the technology represents a new lease on life. A book in low supply can be downloaded from electronic storage and digitally printed in the desired amount. An extant copy of an out-of-print book can be acquired from a library, warehouse, or private source, and can be scanned, printed, and digitally stored."* Thus, the bell curve flattens out endlessly and a book need never goes out of print.

Is Print On Demand Right For You?

Without any doubt, POD has created new opportunities for writers by providing an easy and affordable way to publish their own books.

4. You should be considering Print on Demand only if you plan to publish a book, which will also be made available in print. If you plan to make the book available, only as an electronic download then there is no need to consider POD.

Print on Demand may be easy and affordable but will also bring you against a few challenges.

5. One primary concern with POD is marketing. While all books must be vigorously marketed, extra effort is required for POD-published books, because bookstores rarely will stock them and are even reluctant to offer signings with their authors. Generally, you are the one to perform most of the marketing and promotion of your book. Most POD publishing companies though, will offer marketing plans for an extra cost.

6. Another challenge you will be faced with is to get reviewers to look at your book. Since they are overwhelmed with new book submissions, usually they review only the ones sent by a reputable agent / publisher or the author is known.

How to Choose POD Service Provider or e-Publisher

Choosing the right POD Service Provider is a daunting task and requires a lot of research on your part. If you have taken the time to write a book, then it only makes sense that you should take the time to find the right publisher for your work. If you are reading the book it means that you have decided to e-publish your book so make sure that you carefully review e-publishers and POD service providers before making a decision. There are a variety of models of book e-publishing, each with its own advantages and disadvantages.

7. Think ahead and make a list of questions and wants you have regarding your book. You goal will be to find an e-publisher who matches the most of your needs, and gives the best answers to your questions. If you do this right now, you probably won't have to do it again for you next books. Here are some of the issues you should consider in your hunt for an e-publisher.

- **Contracts** - Read the contract very carefully. If possible, have an attorney look over the contract, especially if you have concerns. Look closely at royalties, advances (if any), costs and rights.

  o What rights do you retain in your work?

  o What rights does the publisher take?

  o How many books do you get for your own use and for use as review copies?

  o If you need more, do you get an author discount?

  o How often do you get paid royalties?

  o Can you get out of the contract if the company doesn't fulfill its obligations or if a mainstream publisher picks-up your book and wants to print it?

  o Where will your book be available?

- How much will you be charged for extra services (cover design, proof reading, editing, marketing, etc)?

- **Formatting**
  - In what type of format must you submit your work?
  - Can you check for errors before the final publication?
  - Can you make changes?
  - How do you submit cover art, author photos and other information?
  - Can you use your own ISBN numbers?
  - How much control do you have over cover design, interior design, typefaces and other parts of the book?

- **Editing**
  - Are the books edited or proofread before they are printed?
  - Are there any additional fees charged for editing or proofreading?
  - If editing services are offered, who are the editors?
  - What experience do they have?
  - Can you get a sample of their work to get a feel for the quality of the editing?

- **Company Background**
  - How long has the company been in business? Although Internet companies are new and exciting, many of them won't last. Be

sure to review carefully the company's background.

o Does the company appear stable so it will be available in the years to come? – In fact, this is a very important issue, especially if you are using ISBN provided by the company. Since the company takes the orders, if there is no more company how will you sell your book?

o Does the company deliver its promises?

o Are there any unexpected costs, unannounced policy changes, loss of rights, marketing disappointments or unsatisfactory products?

- **Other Books Published by the Company**

   o How many books has the company published?

   o How well have those books performed in the market?

   o Is the printing and binding decent? Especially if you have photographs on your book, print quality is essential for its success. Would you be proud to present and sell your book when published by the company? If not, move on.

- **Promotional benefits** - Although marketing and promotion is mostly your responsibility, it's better to get some help on this department by the publisher.

   o Do they promote their authors?

   o Do they contact the media for you?

- o Do they compensate you for any promotional expenses?

- o Do they offer online chats on their website?

- o Do they have a media contact list or a mailing list where you can announce your book?

- o How are review copies handled?

- o How does the publisher feature its most recent releases?

- **Book covers** - Book cover graphics as explained in Chapter 6 play a very important role in your book's success. A killer cover design can help your book stand out and increase sales. So it is important that the e-publisher provides attractive covers, or if not, find out if there is a way you can submit your own cover art.

- **Blurb, sample chapter and synopsis**

  - o Who writes the book synopsis for marketing purposes?

  - o Can the publisher help you find another author to blurb your book?

  - o Does your contract allow you to use part of your work for marketing?

  - o Will the publisher display a sample chapter in their online bookstore?

- **Book price**

  - o How much will your book cost?

  - o How much will readers have to pay for your book?

- How does it compare to the price of other books with similar subject?

- If the e-publisher has deals with retailers, will the price of your book differ there than it does at the e-publisher's bookstore?

- **Delivery time**

  - How long does it take your book to be published after you have signed the contract and submitted all the files?

  - How long does it take the e-publisher to deliver purchased books to consumers? Are delivery times consistent?

- **Retail partners**

  - Who are the e-publisher's retail partners?

  - Does the publisher have agreements with Amazon.com, BN.com and/or Borders.com?

  - What price will readers have to pay for your book at these retailers?

  - Is there a discount or co-op available?

  - How long will it take your book to be delivered to customers? A slow delivery time is a real turn-off to readers.

- **Online bookstore**

  - How does the publisher promote the books?

  - Do they have a bookstore on their website?

  - Is it hard to find?

  - Does it get much traffic?

  - Does it have a bestseller list?

o   Does the bookstore have secure online ordering?

o   Does the publisher have many ordering and payment options? A great online bookstore is essential, especially if you are sending people to the website to buy your book.

- **Sales**

    o   Will you have access to sales information?

    o   How often is it updated?

    o   If there is an online bookstore, can you find out how many people have accessed your book's page or description?

- **Troubleshooting** - If you have a problem or question, is there someone available by email or phone? Is there a support area on the website?

8. It's almost impossible to find the answers to all the questions, but try to find as many as possible. Identify the most important ones for you and look them up. As you network with other writers and do your own research, you will probably be able to find more answers quicker. After putting in some solid research time, you should be able to choose an e-publisher with confidence.

9. In your quest for the right e-publisher, there is only one rule: "DO NOT RUSH!" During your research, you will contact a number of companies who will bombard you with time-limited offers. No matter how great an offer sounds, DO NOT RUSH!

10. Prepare a worksheet to assist you in your research. Try to find as much information as you can for each company, to ensure you have made the right choice.

Conclusion

Print on Demand is very hot right now; in a sense, it is a good intermediary step between the regular method of printing paper books and electronic books. For many writers, POD offers the best of two worlds. Since books are printed only when ordered, POD publishing avoids the massive up-front cost of printing several thousand copies. Customers, however, can still obtain a hard copy of a book, complete with a professional cover and a well designed layout.

POD will help you to have a published book to sell, instead of continually opening rejection letters. Assuming you were accepted into "the published-authors club", it may take up to three years to have a book on the street. POD will get your book to your readers much faster. The list of POD pros could go on, but you get the picture.

CHAPTER 10

32 Online Selling Tips

Promotion and Marketing

1. **Rule #1** - Do not use spam e-mail marketing methods. Instead, use targeted marketing campaigns where people have a chance to opt-in.

2. If you are looking for a quick way to jumpstart website traffic or boost sales, you can buy advertising space in an established newsletter or use one of the known pay-per-click programs.

3. Always keep in mind that the success of your book will depend heavily on your ability to promote it yourself. Publishers are usually busy and most of the time they will only devote the minimum amount of resources and efforts for your book's promotion.

4. If you want your marketing efforts to be successful, you must do a little market research first. For a self published

author such as yourself there are 3 free market research tools that you can use to your advantage:

- Bookstores - You can get useful information about the demand on a book just by looking at the publish date in conjunction with the print number. If a book has been published in the last 12 months and it's already in the third or even higher printing, it's a good indication that the book is selling well.

- Libraries - Visit often your local library and check out the frequency of book check-outs. This is a good indication on the book or subject demand.

- Best Seller Lists - Every publishing house and bookstore (online and offline) have best seller lists. You can even find them in newspapers or magazines. Use them to determine broad trends in title demand.

5. A separate website for your book is a vital part of your marketing efforts. Large bookstores, both online and offline have thousands of titles, so it's very easy and most likely to happen, for your book to get lost among all those titles. With a separate website, you will be able to target every available resource to your book's promotion and it will be a lot easier to track its success.

6. Use your book and website as a means for establishing an interactive relationship between you, your readers and potential buyers. Ask from people who have bought the book to provide you with testimonials and reviews through your website. This way you encourage more people into buying your book.

7. Use every available free method for promoting your website, such as search engines and directories, link ex-

changes (but be careful about the websites you choose) and discussion groups.

8. Do not start hunting for links until you have a web presence that is worth linking to.

9. When starting out, write some content – free – for an authoritative website in order to get a link back to your website.

10. Search for blogs or forums with discussion topics related to your book and if you can make a meaningful addition to the discussion, go ahead and don't forget to include a link to your website.

11. Do not forget press releases. Many websites will let you submit your press release either free or for a small fee. Start with the free ones. Keep in mind that the Internet is the first place reporters look for information.

12. Additionally you can use passive marketing methods to promote your book. This means that you have to pay for advertising. Limit your efforts only to online advertising, because it's the only form of advertising, which allows you to track results efficiently.

13. Share advertising costs with other people. For this, use affiliate marketing. Sign up as a seller on affiliate websites such as clickbank.com or cj.com. You have to be prepared to pay a commission percentage to your affiliates.

Selling

14. One of the best ways to promote your book and increase sales is to distribute one ore two sample chapters, which will act as teasers and make people want to read more. Just like in bookstores people like to browse through books before they buy them, so that they can be sure that they have what they are looking for.

15. Don't forget to include a "Buy Now" link to all of your website's pages.

16. In order to make any sales your website must be set up for online sales. You can do this in two ways:

    - You can redirect your potential buyers to the POD Publisher's sales page of your book, or

    - You can set up a PayPal account for yourself and start accepting payments immediately. Setting up a PayPal account is very easy, it doesn't require any special knowledge, you don't have to worry about safety and hackers since all customer data are stored in their (very) secure servers.

17. Build an opt-in mailing list from existing buyers. This can be done through the "Thank You" page. If you do not spam your mailing list members, they may turn out to be the first buyers of your next book. Make sure you have a privacy policy clearly stated in the signup page.

18. One sure way to increase sales and your credibility is to offer a guarantee and have a money-back policy.

19. Sell your book(s) through multiple websites.

The Website

20. Try to pick a domain based on your book's title rather than your name. If you have picked a great title, it will be a lot easier for people to remember the title, rather than your name.

21. A domain based on your book's title will also help you in your Search Engine Optimization (SEO) efforts, since people will most likely search information relevant to your book's title, rather than your name.

22. You don't have to know many tricks or have special skills

to develop a successful website. A successful website must be attractive to search engines and be able to serve its visitors. Here are some things you need to do to make your website successful:

- Choose the right title for each page of your website. The title is the text that appears between the title tags (<title>, </title>).

- Repeat the words in your title a sufficient amount of times in your body text and headings too, without artificially increasing the keyword density, because search engines will know and will penalize your website.

- Ask your friends and family which keywords and phrases they would use if they were looking for information related to your book's subject and use them to optimize your web pages. You can also use some free online tools available today that give you the amount of times a particular word or phrase has been searched.

- Don't cover too many subjects in a single web page. Instead, break them down to multiple pages. Search engines will love it and your visitors too, since they won't need to scroll endless pages to find the information they need.

23. Offer a media "press kit" through your website. Create a virtual press room in your website where reporters will be able to find scanned images from your book, your bio and more information on the book.

24. The two most critical components of any website are content and contact (the 2 C's). Content refers to the written material found in the website while contact refers to means to contact the owner provided by the website to

its visitors.

25. Don't forget to build your website for speed, so try to avoid flash intros and large images.

26. Your website must establish and enhance your credibility. Use the following guidelines:

   • How to make your website look professional:

      ○ Maintain a pleasing visual design that remains consistent through all the website's pages.

      ○ Keep your layout clean and readable.

      ○ Avoid unnecessary clutter.

      ○ Use proper spelling and grammar.

      ○ Use a common, easy-to-read font.

   • Provide offline and online contact information.

   • Include a privacy statement.

   • Include testimonials.

27. Building a website for an author, such as yourself, is not about technology or aesthetics, it's about content and the only person who can provide the right content is you.

28. Start building your website as soon as possible. A website doesn't have to be "finished" and you can always work on improving or adding content on your spare time.

29. Websites actually benefit from aging, so start as soon as possible.

30. Offer products, services or even a short e-mail course related to your book. This way you earn people's trust and you build up a mailing list, which might come in handy in your next book. Remember to include a privacy statement when you ask for peoples e-mail addresses.

31. Keep the website design clean and simple. Provide all the necessary information and use an easy navigation system. Make the website easy for the search engines to index, so it would be a good idea to avoid the use of flash or other similar technologies.

32. It's a good idea to have a members section for the people who have bought your book. People need to have a sense of belonging somewhere like being members of a small community like yours. In your members section you can offer personal advice, information and updates related to your book and so on. This will boost your credibility and your sales.

How to Find Topics from What You Already Know

This is an exercise for identifying subjects/topics, which you can easily write about, based on what you already know.

1. Take a large sheet of paper (the largest you can find).

2. Divide the paper into 2 columns. Make the left column narrower, but wide enough to incorporate a few words of your writing.

3. In the left hand column write down every topic you can think of, that you already know something about. Leave 7-8 empty lines between each topic. Generating a list of topics you already know something about is easy, here a

few ideas for finding such topics:

- What job do you have?
- What skills do you use in your job?
- What job did you have one, two, three, four, five, etc., years ago?
- What skills did you use in those jobs?
- What did you study in school or college?
- What types of factual TV Programs do you like to watch?
- What types of magazines do you like to read?
- What types of (non-fiction) books do you like to read?
- What types of Internet sites do you like to visit?
- What computer programs do you know well?
- What domestic skills do you have? (Home-making, Home Improvement, Gardening, etc.)
- Do you have an artistic skill? (Music, painting, drawing, etc.)
- What types of major purchases (cars, travel, house) have you made?
- Have you ever had a good deal when buying something?
- What types of things have you sold?
- What things or projects have you made? (Do-it-yourself, construction, electronics, etc.)
- Are you able to fix broken items?
- Do you have pets?

- Are you a parent? If yes, for which parenting issues do you have views or insights?

- Are you into sports or fitness?

- What hobbies do you have now?

- What hobbies did you have one, two, three, four, five, etc., years ago?

- When family or friends ask for your help, what kind of things do they ask you about?

- Where do you live - do you know your local area well?

- Where did you go on your last few vacations?

4. Try to work at a fast pace. Don't stop to evaluate each topic, just write it down and move on to the next one as quickly as possible. Just keep writing more and more topics until you start to get tired - and then take a break.

5. When you finish this, you will end up with a big list. Keep those papers, so you can refer back later, or add more topics.

6. Now, you are going to fill the right column with ideas for Book Topics. Don't worry about exact wording, or the quality of each idea, for now. The key is that you must keep the ideas flowing, and generate as many as possible. So go back to your list of topics that you know something about and try to combine each topic with any of the following, writing down the result in the right-hand column:

- How To ...

- Learn How To ...

- A Beginner's Guide To ...

- An Expert's Guide To ...

- Teach Yourself To …
- It's Easy To …
- Step-by-Step Guide To …
- 99 (or any other number) Tips About …
- Making (Extra) Money
- Saving Money
- Saving Time
- A Complete Guide To …
- Little Known Facts (Secrets) About …

7. Here are some examples:

- How To: "Cook Italian Food" + "How To" = "How To Cook Delicious Italian Meals"
- Learn How To: "Enjoy Calligraphy" + "Learn How To" = "Learn How To Create Beautiful Calligraphic Designs"
- It's Easy To: "Filled In Government Forms In My Job" + "It's Easy To" = "It's Easy To Fill In Tax and Other Forms"
- A Beginner's Guide To: "Use Microsoft Word" + "A Beginner's Guide To" = "A Beginner's Guide To Microsoft Word"
- An Expert's Guide To: "Bake Cakes For Family" + "An Expert's Guide To" = "An Expert's Guide To Making Delicious Cakes"
- Teach Yourself To: "Play Piano" + "Teach Yourself To" = "Teach Yourself to Play the Piano"
- It's Easy To: "Renovated House" + "It's Easy To" = "It's Easy To Renovate Your Old House"

- Step-by-Step Guide To: "Taught My Child To Draw" + "Step-by-Step Guide To Teaching Your Child To Draw"

- 99 Tips About: "Enjoy Gardening" + "99 Tips About" = "99 Tips For A Beautiful Garden"

- Making (Extra) Money: "Make Embroidery" + "Make Money With A Home-based Embroidery Business"

- Saving Money: "Bought A Car" + "Saving Money" = "Save Money When Buying A Car"

- Save Time: "I'm A Home-maker" + "99 Tips About" = "99 Tips For Saving Time On Domestic Chores"

- A Complete Guide To: "Live in New York City" + "A Complete Guide To" = "A Complete Guide To New York City"

- Little Known Facts (Secrets) About: "Enjoy Fishing" + "Secrets" = "Secrets of Catching Bigger Fish"

(Sometimes more than one idea will derive from the same combination, or from combinations of combinations - if this happens, write them all down as sometimes these are the best ideas).

What Makes People Buy

You can't force people to buy a book but you can persuade them to pick your book out from the shelf. "How?" you ask. The answer is quite simple. You have to find those motivational triggers that make people buy. Know their emotions, what they want or fear the most.

Emotions

Emotions are about how people feel or want to feel or don't want to feel. There are two major types of emotions; Desire and Fear. Desire is what we want to achieve in our lives, our work, and our relationships. While on the other hand our fears keep us from getting what we want in life.

As an author you can use these emotions either as a subject for your next book or as marketing material for creating need for your book.

The Top 10 Things That People Want

1. People want to make more money.

2. People want to save money.

3. People want to save time.

4. People want to look better.

5. People want to learn something new.

6. People want to live longer.

7. People want to be comfortable.

8. People want to be loved.

9. People want to be popular.

10. People want to gain pleasure.

The Top 10 Fears that Keep People from Getting What They Want in Life

1. Fear of Failing.

2. Fear of Success.

3. Fear of Being Judged.

4. Fear of Emotional Pain.

5. Fear of Embarrassment.

6. Fear of Being Alone/Abandoned.

7. Fear of Rejection.

8. Fear of Expressing Our True Feelings.

9. Fear of Intimacy.

10. Fear of the Unknown.

Response to Promotional Activities

Recent research has shown which promotional activities led to a purchase. People were allowed to choose more than one activity. These are the results:

Activity	Number of People	Percentage
Previous familiarity with author's other work	466	99.1%
Recommendation of friend	427	90.9%
Reading about book on another person's blog or website	372	79.1%
Cover art	298	63.4%
Reading first chapter of book online or in store	298	63.4%
Reading about book on author's blog or website	296	63.0%
Cover or flap blurbs (promotional quotes)	271	57.7%
Published (print or electronic) book review	263	56.0%
Attending a reading or signing event with author (including a convention)	239	50.9%
Bookseller or librarian recommendation	195	41.5%
Other	37	7.9%
Contest sponsored by author or publisher	33	7.0%
Receiving promotional email from author	30	6.4%
Receiving postcard in mail from author	18	3.8%
Receiving toys or other promotional gimmicks from author	18	3.8%

APPENDIX C

How to Evaluate Web Resources

The following checklists have been developed by Jan Alexander & Marsha Tate.

How to Evaluate an Advocacy Web Page

An Advocacy Web Page is one sponsored by an organization attempting to influence public opinion (that is, one trying to sell ideas). The URL address of the page frequently ends in .org (organization).

Questions to Ask About the Web Page

Note: The greater number of questions listed below answered "yes", the more likely it is you can determine whether the source is of high information quality.

1. Criterion #1: AUTHORITY

   - Is it clear what organization is responsible for the contents of the page?

- Is there a link to a page describing the goals of the organization?

- Is there a way of verifying the legitimacy of this organization? That is, is there a phone number or postal address to contact for more information? (Simply an email address is not enough.)

- Is there a statement that the content of the page has the official approval of the organization?

- Is it clear whether this is a page from the national or local chapter of the organization?

- Is there a statement giving the organization's name as copyright holder?

2. Criterion #2: ACCURACY

- Are the sources for any information clearly listed so they can be verified in another source? (If not, the page may still be useful to you as an example of the ideas of the organization, but it is not useful as a source of information).

- Is the information free of grammatical, spelling, and typographical errors? (These kinds of errors not only indicate a lack of quality control, but also can actually produce inaccuracies in information.)

3. Criterion #3: OBJECTIVITY

- Are the organization's biases clearly stated?

- If there is any advertising on the page, is it clearly differentiated from the informational content?

4. Criterion #4: CURRENCY

- Are there dates on the page to indicate:

When the page was written?

When the page was first placed on the Web?

When the page was last revised?

- Are there any other indications that the material is kept current?

5. Criterion #5: COVERAGE

- Is there an indication that the page has been completed, and is not still under construction?

- Are the topics that the page intends to address clear?

- Does the page succeed in addressing these topics, or has something significant been left out?

- Is the point of view of the organization presented in a clear manner with its arguments well supported?

How to Evaluate a Business/Marketing Web Page

A Business/Marketing Web Page is one sponsored by a commercial enterprise (usually it is a page trying to promote or sell products). The URL address of the page frequently ends in .com (commercial).

Questions to Ask About the Web Page

Note: The greater number of questions listed below answered "yes", the more likely it is you can determine whether the source is of high information quality.

1. Criterion #1: AUTHORITY

- Is it clear what company is responsible for the contents of the page?

- Is there a link to a page describing the nature of the company, who owns the company, and the types of products the company sells?

- Is there a way of verifying the legitimacy of this

company? That is, is there a phone number or postal address to contact for more information? (Simply an email address is not enough.)

- Is there a way of determining the stability of this company?

- Is there a statement that the content of the page has the official approval of the company?

- Is there a statement giving the company's name as copyright holder?

2. Criterion #2: ACCURACY

- Has the company provided a link to outside sources such as product reviews or reports filed with the SEC (the Securities and Exchange Commission) which can be used to verify company claims?

- Are the sources for any information clearly listed so they can be verified in another source?

- Is the information free of grammatical, spelling, and typographical errors? (These kinds of errors not only indicate a lack of quality control, but also can actually produce inaccuracies in information.)

3. Criterion #3: OBJECTIVITY

- For any given piece of information, is it clear what the company's motivation is for providing it?

- If there is any advertising on the page, is it clearly differentiated from the informational content?

4. Criterion #4: CURRENCY

- Are there dates on the page to indicate:

When the page was written?

When the page was first placed on the Web?

When the page was last revised?

- Are there any other indications that the material is kept current?

- For financial information, is there an indication it was filed with the SEC and is the filing date listed?

- For material from the company's annual report, is the date of the report listed?

5. Criterion #5: COVERAGE

- Is there an indication that the page has been completed, and is not still under construction?

- If describing a product, does the page include an adequately detailed description of the product?

- Are all of the company's products described with an adequate level of detail?

- Is the same level of information provided for all sections or divisions of the company?

How to Evaluate a News Web Page

A News Web Page is one whose primary purpose is to provide extremely current information. The URL address of the page usually ends in .com (commercial).

Questions to Ask About the Web Page

Note: The greater number of questions listed below answered "yes", the more likely it is you can determine whether the source is of high information quality.

1. Criterion #1: AUTHORITY

- Is it clear what company or individual is responsible for the contents of the page?

- Is there a link to a page describing the goals of the company?

- Is there a way of verifying the legitimacy of the company? That is, is there a phone number or postal address to contact for more information? (Simply an email address is not enough.)

- Is there a non-Web equivalent version of this material, which would provide a way of verifying its legitimacy?

- If the page contains an individual article, do you know who wrote the article and his or her qualifications for writing on this topic?

- Is it clear who is ultimately responsible for the content of the material?

- Is there a statement giving the company's name as copyright holder?

2. Criterion #2: ACCURACY

- Are sources for information clearly listed so they can be verified in another source?

- Are there editors monitoring the accuracy of the information being published?

- Is the information free of grammatical, spelling, and typographical errors? (These kinds of errors not only indicate a lack of quality control, but also can actually produce inaccuracies in information.)

3. Criterion #3: OBJECTIVITY

- Is the informational content clearly separated from the advertising and opinion content?

- Are the editorials and opinion pieces clearly labeled?

4. Criterion #4: CURRENCY

- Is there a link to an informational page, which describes how frequently the material is updated?

- Is there an indication of when the page was last updated?

- Is there a date on the page to indicate when the page was placed on the Web?

  o If it's a newspaper, does it indicate what edition of the paper the page belongs to?

  o If it's a broadcast, does it indicate the date and time the information on the page was originally broadcast?

5. Criterion #5: COVERAGE

- Is there a link to an informational page, which describes the coverage of the source?

- If you are evaluating a newspaper page and there is a print equivalent, is there an indication of whether the Web coverage is more or less extensive than the print version?

How to Evaluate an Informational Web Page

An Informational Web Page is one whose purpose is to present information. The URL Address frequently ends in .edu or .gov, as many of these pages are sponsored by educational institutions or government agencies.

Questions to Ask About the Web Page

Note: The greater number of questions listed below answered "yes", the more likely it is you can determine whether the source is of high information quality.

1. Criterion #1: AUTHORITY

- Is it clear who is responsible for the contents of the page?

- Is there a link to a page describing the purpose of the sponsoring organization?

- Is there a way of verifying the legitimacy of the page's sponsor? That is, is there a phone number or postal address to contact for more information? (Simply an email address is not enough.)

- Is it clear who wrote the material and are the author's qualifications for writing on this topic clearly stated?

- If the material is protected by copyright, is the name of the copyright holder given?

2. Criterion #2: ACCURACY

- Are the sources for any information clearly listed so they can be verified in another source?

- Is the information free of grammatical, spelling, and typographical errors? (These kinds of errors not only indicate a lack of quality control, but also can actually produce inaccuracies in information.)

- Is it clear who has the ultimate responsibility for the accuracy of the content of the material?

- If there are charts and/or graphs containing statistical data, are the charts and/or graphs clearly labeled and easy to read?

3. Criterion #3: OBJECTIVITY

- Is the information provided as a public service?

- Is the information free of advertising?

- If there is any advertising on the page, is it clearly differentiated from the informational content?

4. Criterion #4: CURRENCY

- Are there dates on the page to indicate:
  - o When the page was written?
  - o When the page was first placed on the Web?
  - o When the page was last revised?
- Are there any other indications that the material is kept current?
- If material is presented in graphs and/or charts, is it clearly stated when the data was gathered?
- If the information is published in different editions, is it clearly labeled what edition the page is from?

5. Criterion #5: COVERAGE

- Is there an indication that the page has been completed, and is not still under construction?
- If there is a print equivalent to the Web page, is there a clear indication of whether the entire work is available on the Web or only parts of it?
- If the material is from a work, which is out of copyright (as is often the case with a dictionary or thesaurus), has there been an effort to update the material to make it more current?

How to Evaluate a Personal Web Page

A Personal Web Page is one published by an individual who may or may not be affiliated with a larger institution. Although the URL address of the page may have a variety of endings (e.g. .com, .edu, etc.), a tilde (~) is frequently embedded somewhere in the URL.

Questions to Ask About the Web Page

Note: The greater number of questions listed below answered "yes", the more likely it is you can determine whether the source is of high information quality.

1. Criterion #1: AUTHORITY

   - Is it clear what individual is responsible for the contents of the page?

   - Does the individual responsible for the page indicate his or her qualifications for writing on this topic?

   - Is there a way of verifying the legitimacy of this individual? (Because it is difficult to verify the legitimacy of an individual, personal home pages may be a useful source for personal opinion but use extreme caution when using them as a source for information.)

2. Criterion #2: ACCURACY

   - Are the sources for any information clearly listed so they can be verified in another source? (If not, the page may still be useful to you as an example of the ideas of the individual, but it is not useful as a source of information.)

   - Is the information free of grammatical, spelling, and typographical errors? (These kinds of errors not only indicate a lack of quality control, but also can actually produce inaccuracies in information.)

3. Criterion #3: OBJECTIVITY

   - Are the person's biases clearly stated?

4. Criterion #4: CURRENCY

   - Are there dates on the page to indicate:

     o When the page was written?

When the page was first placed on the Web?

When the page was last revised?

- Are there any other indications that the material is kept current?

5. Criterion #5: COVERAGE

- Is there an indication that the page has been completed, and is not still under construction?

Research Beyond Google: 14 Research Resources

1. **Artcyclopedia (http://www.artcyclopedia.com/)** - Information on artists or art movements. The site provides links to museums worldwide where works by over 8,200 artists can be viewed. While most of the artists listed are painters and sculptors, you can also find photographers, decorative artists, and architects.

2. **BioMedCentral (http://www.biomedcentral.com/)** - An archive of over 170 biology, chemistry and medical journals. The articles published on BioMedCentral are all peer-reviewed to ensure that they are accurate and appropriate for use as reference materials. A majority of the

materials linked to on the site is free, but a few journals do require a subscription service to access.

3. **Digital History (http://www.digitalhistory.uh.edu/)** – Provides information on U.S. history, as well as essays on film, private life, and science and technology, and visual histories about Lincoln's America and America's Reconstruction. The site also makes use of primary sources such as gravestones, historical advertising, and letters to give a more vivid picture of American History. The site also includes numerous reference materials including an extensive audio-visual archive.

4. **FindArticles.com (http://findarticles.com/)** - Browse articles from about 500 print periodicals starting in 1998. Usage is completely free of charge.

5. **INFOMINE (http://infomine.ucr.edu/)** - INFOMINE is a virtual library of Internet resources. It contains useful tools such as databases, electronic journals, electronic books, bulletin boards, mailing lists, online library card catalogs, articles, and directories of researchers.

6. **Internet History Sourcebooks**
    (http://www.fordham.edu/halsall) - A collection of public domain and copy permitted historical texts. Topics include ancient, medieval, modern, women's, and Islamic history among others.

7. **Internet Public Library (http://www.ipl.org/)** - The library is a collection of online resources that are organized by subject, everything from accounting to social sciences.

8. **Intute (http://www.intute.ac.uk/)** - Provides access to Web-based resources for science, technology, arts, humanities, and social sciences. The database contains well over 100,000 records and continues to grow.

9. **Librarians Internet Index (http://lii.org/)** - The Librarians Internet Index is a Website created and maintained by a group of librarians, very similar to the Internet Public Library. It has a searchable directory of Internet resources, on a wide variety of topics.

10. **Library of Congress (http://www.loc.gov/index.html)** - Contains a wealth of materials on American history including photos, maps, documents, and even sheet music. In addition, the site offers online exhibits

11. **Perseus Digital Library**

    (http://www.perseus.tufts.edu/) - This digital library provides information on the ancient world, including archaeology, atlas, texts and translations as well as English Renaissance and the American Civil War.

12. **Project Gutenberg**

    (http://www.gutenberg.org/wiki/Main_Page)   - Project Gutenberg, provides web access to over 20,000 books. It is the largest collection of free books on the internet.

13. **Research Guide for Students**

    (http://www.aresearchguide.com/) - Provides guidelines for the technical aspects of writing a paper such as layout and style guides as well as a plethora of links to other research resources on just about every topic imaginable.

14. **U.S. Government Manual**

    (http://www.gpoaccess.gov/gmanual/index.html)   - Provides comprehensive information on the agencies of the legislative, judicial, and executive branches as well as semi-official agencies, international organizations in which the United States participates, and boards, commissions, and committees. It also includes the basics of U.S. governmental documents: the Declaration of Independence and the Constitution.

(Found at **Online Education Database - http://oedb.org**)

Color and Book Cover Design: A Reference Chart

Color	Positive Meaning	Negative Meaning	Spiritual Meaning
Black	Cleverness	Evil	
	Dignified	Depression	
	Hipness		
	Mystery		
	Prestige		
	Sexuality		
	Sophisticated		
	Wit		
	Worldly		

Color	Positive Meaning	Negative Meaning	Spiritual Meaning
Blue	Confident	Demanding	Forgiveness
	Conservative	Perfectionism	Healing
	Cool		Meditation
	Harmony		Tranquility
	Love		
	Patience		
	Peace		
	Peace		
	Perseverance		
	Reliable		
	Sensitive		
	Serenity		
	Social		
	Tranquility		
	Trusting		
	Vulnerable		
Brown	Comfort		
	Down-to-earth		
	Duty		
	Family		
	Harmony		
	Hearth		
	Home		
	Loyal		
	Quality		
	Reliable		
	Responsibility		
	Security		
	Sense of belonging		
	Simplicity		
	Stability		
	Steady		
	Strong		
	Substance		
	Understanding		

Color	Positive Meaning	Negative Meaning	Spiritual Meaning
Green	Balance	Careful	Fertility
	Caring	Conventional	Healing
	Concerned	Envy	Luck
	Fastidious	Gossip	Money
	Generous		Prosperity
	Good citizen		
	High morality		
	Intelligent		
	Involved		
	Kind		
	Loyal		
	Sensitive		
	Stable		
Grey	Balanced	Boring	
	Calm	Depression	
	composed	Fear	
	Conservative	Indifferent	
	Cool	Restless	
	Hardworking		
	Neutral		
	Noncommittal		
	Practical		
	Reliable		
	Safe		
	Secure		
	Status quo		
Orange	Adventurous	Fickle	Attraction
	Agreeable	Undependable	Authority
	Bright		Joy
	Determination		Strength
	Expansive		Success
	Extroverted		
	Good-natured		
	Unique		
	Vibrant		

Color	Positive Meaning	Negative Meaning	Spiritual Meaning
	Warm		
Pink	Beauty	Overly feminine	
	Calm	Prissy	
	Caring	Red with the passion removed	
	Charm		
	Delicacy		
	Even-keeled		
	Intuitive		
	Non-violent		
	Refined		
	Refinement		
	Reserved		
	Romance		
	Romantic		
	Sensitive		
	Sophisticated		
	Sweetness		
	Tenderness		
	Warmth		
	Well-bred		
Purple	Artists	Conflicting	Psychic awareness
	Charming	Moody	Spirituality
	Creative	Secretive	Wisdom
	Different		
	Enigmatic		
	Generous		
	Intrigue		
	Keen observation		
	Mystery		
	Sensitivity		
	Spiritual		
	Unconventional		
	Vanity		
	Wit		

Color	Positive Meaning	Negative Meaning	Spiritual Meaning
Red	Competitive	Impatient	Courage
	Daring	Opinionated	Energy
	Exciting	Restless	Enthusiasm
	Fire		Love
	Heat		Passion
	Impossible to ignore		
	Intense		
	Passion		
	Stimulating		
	Zest		
Yellow	Ambitious	Aloof	Clairvoyance
	Artistic	Egotistical	Communication
	Challenge	Perfectionistic	Learning
	Creative	Shy	Mind
	Idealistic		
	Imaginative		
	Inquiring minds		
	Loves novelty		
	Luminous		
	Optimistic		
	Original		
	Reliable		
	Spiritual		
	Sunshine		
	Warm		
White	Blinding	Critical	Peace
	Bright	Fussy	Protection
	Cautious	Sterile	Purity
	Clean	Uptight	Truth
	Cleanliness		
	Fresh		
	Immaculate		
	Innocence		
	Neat		
	Purity		

Color	Positive Meaning	Negative Meaning	Spiritual Meaning
	Purity		
	Self-sufficient		
	Shrewd		
	Simplicity		
	Snow		
	Youth		

How to Write a Press Release for Your Book

Your very first action in your marketing efforts should be the press release. A press release is the most cost effective and immediate way to "get the word out" and create a buzz about your new book.

A press release is a brief announcement towards the media – newspapers, magazines, radio, TV and news websites – which informs them of something new and newsworthy.

You should be careful when writing a press release not to make it sound like an advertisement or an article because it is not. The press release is a news item, which needs to get the attention of the right people, usually journalists that will pick it up and publish it.

Your press release must have the proper format and include the right information in order to be noticed.

How Long Should a Press Release Be?

Remember that you are writing a news item and not a novel, so keep it short. A 400-600 word press release should be enough. Never write press releases more than 800 words long.

How to Format the Press Release

The very first line of the press release should be written in capital letters and indicate the time when the release will be effective. It should be something like "FOR IMMEDIATE RELEASE" or "FOR RELEASE ON [DATE]".

Below you should put your **contact information** or the **main text** of the press release. As a rule of thumb, based on survey conducted to journalists, if you are sending the press release electronically continue with the body text; If you are sending the press release by fax or mail put your contact information next. The contact information should include the name of the contact person by name, PR firm (if any) or company where contact person works; then phone number, and e-mail address. Each item should be on a separate line.

Your next line should be the **identifier line**, which indicates the target audience of the press release. It should be in the form of: Category/Subcategory (i.e. "Business/Publications").

The next element of the press release, right below the identifier line, should be the **headline**. The purpose of the headline is to grab the reader's attention so it must be short, simple and effective. The headline must describe a newsworthy event, like the release of a new book and state clearly what you intend to announce through your press release. Look in newspapers for headlines that grab your attention and produce something similar. The headline must be less than 30 words. If you absolutely have to use a longer headline, divide it into headline and sub-headline.

After the headline, write the **body** of the press release. This is the actual story that you want to share with the world and must contain everything the potential editor/journalist will need to know in order to publish your press release.

The first sentence of the first paragraph should be your location in capital letters followed by the date of the news announcement, which is always the date that the news will be distributed.

The first paragraph is also the place where the URL of your website should be placed.

The rest of the paragraphs should describe what your book is about. At least one paragraph should describe a feature or benefit while the rest paragraphs should be a quotation from an expert or someone significant who will describe how the market will benefit from your book. This will help to bring a human feeling to the press release and put a face on the story.

It's important to use good formatting. Use small paragraphs clearly separated which will make the press release easier to scan.

The headline and the first paragraph should clearly state who is announcing what.

Use the last paragraph for a short bio of yourself. Talk about your accomplishments and other books you have published. Establish your expertise in the field and demonstrate that you are qualified to be writing about your book's subject. Be sure you include some human-interest features, professional associations, or club memberships.

The last line, which can be by itself or as part of the last sentence should be your website's URL where the editor/journalist can find more information.

Below this line, you may include a photo (i.e. the cover of your book) and a link where it can be found.

If you haven't placed your contact information at the top of the press release, place them now.

Finally, you need to close the press release with three hash marks

(###), which indicate the end of the release.

A Few Writing Guidelines

Write the first paragraph as precise and to the point as possible since a great number of newspapers use the first paragraph as a summary of the press release.

Remember that the press release is not an advertisement, so avoid phrases like "This is the best book that you will ever read…"

Make sure that you have covered the "5 W's" of journalism: Who, What, When, Where, and Why. Include some benefit statements about the book: Who endorses the book? Include quotes or blurbs. What makes your book new, different, and notable? When is your next book signing? Where is the book available? What is the book's price and ISBN? Why should someone read it? You get the picture!

It's often wise to post a "book summary" at the end of the release comprising the name of the publisher, the author, the book title, the ISBN number(s) and related format (such as hardcover, 250pp), and publication date.

Review and edit your press release as you have done with your book. Look for grammatical and spelling errors. Print out the press release and read it aloud. Make sure the meanings are clear and that the press release makes sense.

Make sure when you submit your press release that any special characters, like trademarks, which you may have used appear correctly and not as gargled text.

The above guidelines should you to compose and submit a proper release, which fits the criteria of what editors are looking for. This will ensure your best chance of getting the invaluable free publicity, which only the print and electronic media outlets can provide.

Example Press Releases

FOR IMMEDIATE RELEASE

Of interest to editors and journalists covering:
Books, Publishing, Libraries, Poetry

New Poetry Book is Released by Michelle True

(PRWEB) February 10, 2005 -- Michelle Ailene True is proud
to announce the release of her second book of poetry. "True
Emotions" has an official release date of March 17, 2005
but it is available for pre-order now on www.amazon.com,
www.barnesandnoble.com,   www.booksamillion.com   and
www.publishamerica.com.

True Emotions has received numerous positive reviews to
date and contains poems about various subjects such as relationships, moving forward in life, how the process of
writing feels like for a writer, homelessness, war, di-
vorce, parenthood, and other issues.

Michelle's mission is to help promote poetry in the north
and northwest suburbs of Chicago. To that end, she founded
and operates Poetic License Writers Group, which meets at
the Indian Trails Library in Wheeling once a month. She also   founded   and   operates   True   Poet   Magazine
(www.truepoetmagazine.com).

As Poetry Editor for "The Professional Author Newsletter"
she write a monthly column ("The Published Poet") in which
she provides tips for how poets can improve their writing
skills, find new poetry markets and get published. She has
been interviewed in several radio talk shows, and for several newspaper articles. She was selected as the Featured
Writer for June 2004 by PoeticVoices, an award-winning Internet-based poetry magazine.

She mentors high school students interested in a writing
career and is a member of several local, state and national
literary organizations.

To arrange for an interview or schedule a poetry reading,
call Michelle at XXX-XXX-XXXX or visit her website at
www.michelleailenetrue.com.

###

FOR IMMEDIATE RELEASE

Instant Book Writing Kit – How To Write, Publish and Market Your Own Money-Making Book (or eBook) Online - New eBook Upstages Traditional Book Publishing Model With New "Online Publishing Model"

A newly released ebook says the traditional book publishing industry operates an archaic and dysfunctional business model that exploits small time authors and publishers. According to the author, Shaun Fawcett, his Instant Book Writing Kit offers a new "online publishing model" that shows independent authors and publishers how to use multiple online distribution channels (via the Internet) to bypass the conventional publishing model and make a lot more money for their efforts.

(PRWEB) June 28, 2004 -- A newly released ebook says the traditional book publishing industry operates an archaic and dysfunctional business model that exploits small time authors and publishers. According to the author, Shaun Fawcett, his Instant Book Writing Kit offers a new "online publishing model" that shows independent authors and publishers how to use multiple online distribution channels (via the Internet) to bypass the conventional publishing model and make a lot more money for their efforts.

"I was shocked when I published my first two books using the traditional book publishing model a few years ago. Even though I had by-passed the major publishing houses by self-publishing, I wasn't able to completely side-step the way that industry operates, since I still had to adhere to its operating practices in order to get my books into the bookstores. I was stunned to learn about the archaic and exploitive nature of many of the standard business practices still used by the book publishing industry in North America".

Fawcett says it was largely the dubious business practices of the traditional publishing industry that motivated him to find a better way to publish and market his own books. He claims that he has done exactly that, and has now documented his new approach to publishing -- the Online Publishing Model -- in detail in his newly released Instant Book Writing Kit. His Kit offers a step-by-step system for writing, publishing, and marketing a book or ebook using Internet-based distribution channels that almost completely by-passes the traditional publishing infrastructure.

"One of the most blatant examples of these unacceptable practices is when the industry forces authors/self-publishers to wait a full 90 to 120 days, and sometimes longer, to get paid after a book sale is made" stated Faw-cett. "Another example is the industry's standard protocol for 'returns' whereby book sellers are given 100% refunds for books they order but do not sell, and then these re-funds get charged back to the author, often months after the initial transaction!" He went on to add, "But the most mind-boggling and little known fact is how that industry victimizes small time authors and self-publishers by paying them the measly sum of between 3% and 6% of the cover price of their own book – in my opinion, that borders on crimi-nal."

According to the Fawcett, Instant Book Writing Kit is a step-by-step instruction manual that explains exactly how he went about writing, publishing and marketing 7 success-ful ebooks over a 27-month period. He claims that if you follow his 17 Action Steps To Online Publishing Success you will significantly increase your book/ebook sales and prof-its over what they would be with the traditional publishing model.

"Through this ebook, I am giving independent authors and self-publishers direct access to a more profitable way to write, publish and market their books/ebooks based on my own hard-earned, trial-and error learning experiences over a three-year period."

Instant Book Writing Kit, is the seventh in a series of ebooks that Fawcett has released in the past 34 months. His other ebooks include: Instant Home Writing Kit (2001), In-stant Recommendation Letter Kit (2002), Instant Business Letter Kit (2002), Instant Resignation Letter Kit (2003), Instant Reference Letter Kit (2003), and Instant College Admission Essay Kit (2003).

This new ebook can be viewed at:
http://www.instantbookwritingkit.com

Shaun Fawcett is Web Master of a popular writing help Web site, www.writinghelp-central.com. Every week, thousands of people visit that site to obtain tips, advice, and resource information on their everyday writing needs including: per-sonal letters, business letters, resumes, cvs, reports, es-says, and term papers. His special Web site dedicated to practical Writing Tools is: www.WritingHelpTools.com

# # #

Media Contact:
Shaun Fawcett:
1-800-600-6550 (toll-free) or info@writinghelptools.com

Please visit and register free at Thomas Kaye's website for more books, information and updates, at:

http://www.thomaskaye.com

Thank you!

791320

Printed in Great Britain by
Amazon.co.uk, Ltd.,
Marston Gate.